The Man's Book

Susan,

&

to you.

With love,

Randy

The Man's Book

101 Ways to Survive Women's Liberation and Other Female Nonsense

Randy T. Smith

Pentland Press, Inc.
England • USA • Scotland

PUBLISHED BY PENTLAND PRESS, INC.
5122 Bur Oak Circle, Raleigh, North Carolina 27612
United States of America
919-782-0281

ISBN 1-57197-089-4
Library of Congress Catalog Card Number 97-075507

Printed in the United States of America

Table of Contents

"I think you're supposed to get shot with an arrow or something, but the rest of it isn't supposed to be so painful."

–Boy, 8

Dedication

I dedicate this to my son, Matthew, and all men that have spent time in the foxhole.

Foreword

As we enter the twenty-first century, the meaning of manhood has evolved into a state of considerable confusion. In part, this confusion is a result of the feminist movement. Some females have become liberated and have "succeeded" in becoming separated and alienated from man. Other women have taken a place of independence and equality in their dealings with men. This has caused man's position in his relationship with women to change, with much more variation and searching in how men and women relate to each other.

Other social and technological changes have added to the confusion. The increasing divorce rate has fractured the family as the foundation of our social structure. The prevalence of serial monogamy (moving from one exclusive partner to another), in and out of marriage, has blurred the morality of commitment between two partners. Technological advance has created new opportunities as we now have video dating services and long-distance relationships via jet, FAX, and e-mail. Taken together, the magnitude and speed of these changes have added to the state of confusion. All of this comes with a cost. We pay an enormous price in personal emotional pain and in safety-net expenses from unhappy, dysfunctional, and broken relationships and families.

This book is written to provide some guideposts to lessen the confusion of man's journey in the new millennium. The book provides one man's response to the feminist movement. It represents, for me, the highest truth of what it is to be a man in our time. You will find many constructive suggestions, but it is not intended to be a final word on the subject. Mix my ideas with your own sense of what works, to achieve your own highest truth. The final word will be your own.

I write this as a guy who has spent time in the foxhole. I am not some guru expounding all your answers from an ivory tower. My view of life comes from loving parents, several good, long-term relationships, two divorces, a variety of dating experiences, two living children, one dead dog, and a spiritual quest to try to make sense of all this. Sundry life experiences and general readings have provided the material for what is written.

My hope is that this will bring love, compassion, and inspiration to you and to those around you. Good luck.

Acknowledgements

I have many people to thank for helping me create this book, although I didn't really create anything. I just wrote about a pathway that was blazed by other writers, enriched by the many people who have blessed my life, and hopefully illuminated by the moonlight and sunlight of some higher being. I put the pen on paper (actually, fingers on keyboard), and something other than me moved it. I am not presumptive enough to say that it was God; some women may contend that it was the devil.

My mother was an original independent woman. She decided one day to leave the security and comfort of life as a housewife and get a job. It was a decision made out of self-respect, not out of necessity. My relationship with her was wonderful. She was my introduction to the concept of love. She gave me the enormous advantage of at least starting life with a wholesome view of women. God bless her.

My father was a good and caring man. When it counted, he was always there for me. He took his responsibilities as a husband and father seriously. He struggled mightily with the idea of my mother getting a job and expressing herself outside the home. To him, that was a personal affront to his role as supreme provider. But she hung in there, and he hung in there with her. God bless him.

My mother and father had an imperfect relationship. Their marriage wasn't easy. But, to their credit, they honored themselves by honoring their commitment to the very end. God bless them.

My former mates and girlfriends have given me the gift of much joy and much pain. I say "gift" because without the pain I never would have had the motivation to write this book. I literally could not have done it without them. Likewise, my female friends and acquaintances have been open-minded enough to support my need to tell this story. Special thanks go to Lorena Goodin and Jean Whitney for their review of sections of the work in progress and their constructive suggestions from a woman's perspective.

My son, Matthew, and several of my male friends provided both encouragement and content for this book. In no small way, this book is a collective male expression. I wish to thank the following men for reading the manuscript, in whole or in part, and providing invaluable feedback. They are: Jim Coghlan, David Dill, Pete Donaghy and Bert England. And special thanks to Norman O'Neill, without whose counsel, this may never have come to print. If she calls any of you on this, just remember—it's all Randy's fault!

I also wish to acknowledge the many writers who have come before me, and have challenged me to move beyond the frustration of life to something better. Many of the authors who provided me with a foundation for what is written here are included in the bibliography.

Finally, I wish to thank the management and staff at Pentland Press. They found the courage to take on this project. What is especially remarkable is that Pentland's letterhead is graced by several women. I thank them for their input, understanding, and professionalism. Working with the Pentland team to get this book into print has been an absolute pleasure.

Creativity is often an evolutionary process of building on others' ideas. I just hope that we, together, can elevate the dance floor, the war zone (as in the battle of the sexes), and the futon to a higher level. Thanks for your help.

The Man's Book

Chapter One

Isn't She Wonderful?

Of course she is wonderful. God made her from our rib. She is Venus, the goddess of love. Man as yin and woman as yang are two opposite forces that complement each other in life. The round peg fits the round hole, as our "zig" complements her "zag." And statistically, if you find a good one, you will live longer with her than you will alone. I'm not sure, however, what the social scientists would find if they conducted comparison testing on man with a good woman, versus man with a good dog, as companion.

Here is a list of activities that you can do with her:

- At times, you can talk to her about the most inane, improbable, and intimate things.
- You can walk down the street, and climb the tallest mountain (or at least a big hill) with her.
- You can take her to a movie, and she can make you dinner, or vice versa.
- You can look at each other in the candlelight with the look that lovers look.
- You, together, can ride a roller coaster, as well as the roller coaster of life.
- You can rub her feet after a long, hard day.
- You can throw her a Frisbee and watch her run for it. Her ability to catch it is not important.
- You can watch her wiggle her toes in the warm sand at the beach.
- You can share champagne and a sunset with her.
- Snuggled closely, you can silently contemplate the meaning of life in the flames of a fire.
- You can roll over and know that she is there.
- You can make love with her.
- You can hold her and bask in the golden glow of the afterglow.
- You can take her hand while she is having your baby.
- You can . . . et cetera, et cetera . . .

I know. This is getting to be a bit much, especially for a man's book. But I wanted to at least start this book on a positive, happy note. She is wonderful—you wouldn't be with her if she wasn't. The beginning of liberation survival is to understand how she charms, enchants, and hooks you in the first place. Most of us will take a good woman over a good dog anytime.

Chapter Two

Liberated From What?

The liberated woman is liberated from what? Let me give you some hints. She is not liberated from doing housework, having babies, raising children, cooking meals, making money, or having a good time. *By intention, she is liberated from you, friend.*

If you don't understand this—if you think that this "sugar and spice and everything nice" is going to be forever devoted to you—you may be in for a big surprise. Most guys start life expressing their love for a female innocently enough. There are sweaty palms just thinking about calling her. Actually, the thought process is secondary to the raging hormones and the need to replace mother's love. The "selection" mechanism for his young love is the female's control of man based on his addiction to her beauty and sexuality. He has been seduced by her manipulation of the questionable intelligence of the penis, which missed altogether her emotional fickleness and ulterior motives. He may initiate the hunt, but she ultimately captures the hunter and domesticates him into her manservant. By the time some blood begins arriving in his cranium, the guy has awakened to emotional and financial devastation.

The only thing that separates love from pain is knowledge. You can get the knowledge from a book or from life's tough experiences. Ideally, you can learn it the easy way, and be spared some of the hard knocks and pain. If your thought processes originate below your waist concerning the role and nature of the female, you will get screwed in more ways than one.

Women are liberated; they are planning to be liberated; or their psychologist is advising them to be liberated. She wants her own job for money, her own car for traveling, and her own boots for walking. Her therapist is telling her that this will bring self-esteem. Liberation is a mind-set that gives her the freedom to say, "I'm out of here," if you don't measure up. Industry, religion, and government love it. She is an abundant source of credit, cars, boots, donations, and taxes. Liberation is a major driving force for many women today.

There is one problem with this that will impact you. When she exercises her right to be liberated and changes her mind, you will be hurt. Her liberation will create a separation and alienation from you that will cause emotional pain and financial hardship. The second way of surviving liberation is to understand it going in, so you can minimize the damage from it coming out.

Remember, she is liberated from you, friend.

Chapter Three

A Woman of Independent Means

There is a silver lining in all this liberation and bra burning business. No, I don't mean its implication for wet T-shirts. Whereas liberated women are separated from man by intention, independent women are something else. Independent women are by definition self-sufficient. They are not dependent on you financially. This is a good thing for many reasons.

How do you feel about a woman who "loves" you so she can get married, get pregnant, and have access to your money? There is an advantage to getting involved with self-sufficient women. If they have their own money, they are less likely to covet yours. They are more likely to love you for who you are. I don't know about you, but I like the idea of being loved for being me.

Men respect women who have their act together. A woman's ability to care for herself is positive for her self-image. She brings her wholeness, not neediness, into the relationship. If she is feeling good about herself, she may be more inclined to feel good about you. This may be the most important reason that her independence is a good thing for us.

Her self-sufficiency relieves you of the pressure of being the sole provider. It may give you a little more room to explore your life's dream. Or the two incomes may give some monetary surplus to move you both further and faster toward financial independence. Or perhaps her income frees you and your income to bring a bit of luxury to her life.

The final reason relates to her prerogative. If she changes her mind about you, she can support herself. That theoretically means that you will not pay alimony if she decides to divorce you.

Are you a macho guy who needs to be the sole provider? You wouldn't be one of those "keep them barefoot and pregnant" types, would you? If so, you may have an unhealthy need for control. Women prefer being seduced, rather than controlled, and the good ones have earned sufficient independence to be able to seek it. The "barefoot" method of control no longer works in our society. Eventually, she will walk barefoot into her divorce attorney's office, and soon you will be the one with bare feet.

I, for one, applaud women's independence. Turn the energy of the women's movement into a positive. The third way to survive liberation is to go with the flow of social change, and find a women of independent means.

Chapter Four

A Woman's Prerogative

A part of women's liberation is her prerogative to change her mind. I just got a call from a lady friend who canceled our dinner date for tomorrow night. Last week, another female friend called, and said that she had changed her plans to visit for the weekend. Two weeks ago, a female acquaintance called to say she wasn't coming for dinner—this with the bread baked, the salad made, and the steaks marinated. And so it goes; this type of thing is typical. If she can't honor her word in the small stuff, what do you think she will do with the major commitments?

Most marriages end in divorce. From my perspective, most marriages end because of a female mind change. It's no wonder that men are cautious about marriage. (Be advised that feminists will replace the word "cautious" with "phobic" here. Whatever word is used to describe it, men are perfectly justified in being fearful of making what may well end up being a one-sided commitment.) As long as it's convenient and fun and fulfilling, she is "committed." When the going gets tough, she calls her girlfriend and then her divorce attorney. Her decision is no-fault, meaning that it can be completely emotional and irrational. The divorce court has cooperated with this. The court has tipped the scale in favor of female child custody, and male child support. Too many divorce lawyers get rich from all this misery. We need a little more commitment to, and compassion for, each other. This female propensity for divorce is just plain wrong, and it is destroying the fabric of American society.

A women's prerogative is humorous when she has a fetish about changing her toenail color. It's not so funny when the sheriff knocks on your door to serve you with her divorce papers. It's not so funny when you make love with her in the evening, and she files a charge of date rape in the morning. It's not so funny when she goes from not wanting to have children to demanding control of her body. Her right to continue the pregnancy is linked to your "right" to provide her with child support. And, of course, we are the bad guys when we don't cheerfully go along with whatever inconvenience or devastation their prerogative may have caused. Don't be confused about this. This is not about male flexibility; it is about female fickleness.

Do understand that women seemingly can't help themselves, when it comes to their prerogative. I am beginning to suspect that this is a part of the female gene structure. The fourth way to survival helps you understand the need to position yourself to minimize damage from her mind changes.

Chapter Five

When She Changes Her Mind

You have been pushed back to your own three yard line. It's fourth down and twenty-five yards to go. You're losing, and half time is coming up. What do you do? What do you do *after* she exercises her female prerogative and changes her mind? You drop back ten yards and punt. You give in, but don't give up.

Be aware that when she changes her mind you are in a no-win situation. When she calls to cancel the date, you are supposed to know that her business deal or her headache or her comfort level is top priority. The concert tickets that you bought or the fresh baked bread that you made are not important. If you object to her female prerogative, you are a one-way jerk. So you do the gentlemanly and gracious thing—you give in.

Please appreciate that when she changes her mind you will get in deeper if you wiggle. We're referring to quicksand here, and not, you know, something else. She calls and says that she is not coming for the weekend, because this relationship with you has no potential. Last week, after the great sex, she thought the relationship had potential. You think it has potential, but this week she's changed her mind. If you go on the defensive (saying, "But I do love you, I do cherish you, I do talk to you, I do respect you . . .") you will piss her off. What's worse, you will be called "boring and egotistical." Don't make a bad situation worse. Take it like a man and punt!

The sad truth is that when she changes her mind, you are forced into damage control. You are not in control. You lost control when you first put yourself in the position of being harmed by her mind change. You have just been served with her divorce papers. She is in a emotional mind set that knows you are the devil himself, straight from hell. You can't reason with female emotion. Her justification for your diabolical, lowlife status is immaterial and unimportant. The longer you wallow in self-defense, the longer you wallow in self-pity. This just prolongs the emotional damage you do to yourself, and her control over your hurt feelings. After considering chapter forty-one, the fifth way to survive liberation is to move on with your life.

Chapter Six

Double Standards

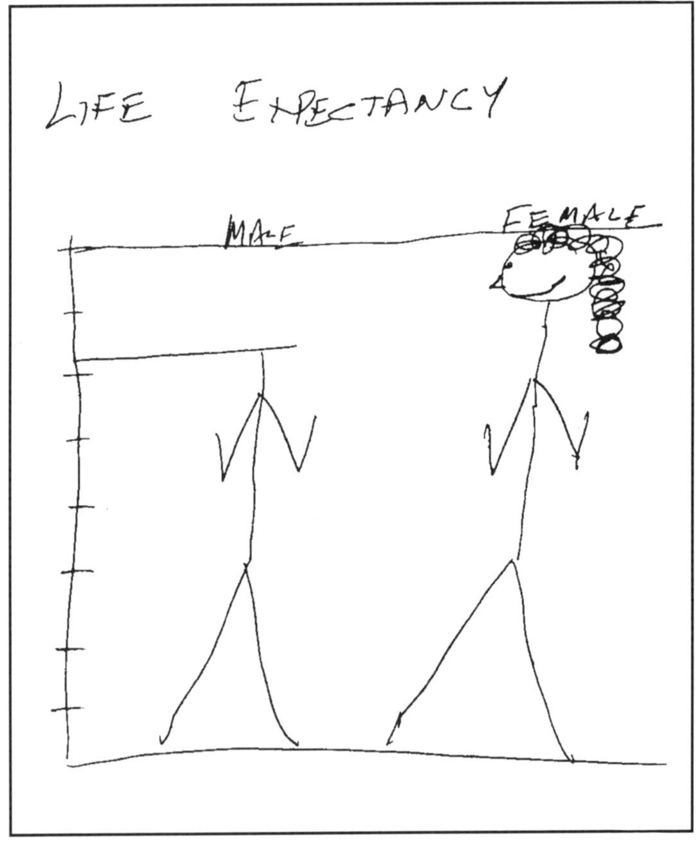

Once upon a time, we had women bitching about the guy with the gut and tattoo as he mutters something about "thunder thighs" and a 2.5 on a scale of 10. Women have demanded equal rights, and have succeeded in equalizing this double standard. Now, we have the lady with the sagging breasts and the tattoo finding liberation from Mr. Couch

Potato with the "love handles." A valid complaint for divorce is now your excessive love handles.

At one time, we had the double standard of calling the promiscuous guy "a stud," and the promiscuous gal "a slut." Fortunately, as a society, we have evolved beyond this double standard. We don't sleep around anymore, do we? This is not necessarily because it is immoral, but because we're fearful of getting some dreaded life-threatening disease.

We have "progressed" to a much bigger and better double standard. It is simply this: she demands all the benefits of the feminist agenda and liberation, and at the same time expects to be treated to all of trappings of an American princess. This means that she expects to be cherished, protected, and pampered. The princess has doors opened, meals and entertainment provided, and all other expenses paid. What is hers is hers, and what is yours is hers. And if you don't play by her standards, it's no sex tonight, you cheap bastard. Or perhaps she'll see you in divorce court to take custody of your children. The man gets to fight for the children; the woman gets the children and the financial support. Afterwards, she expects prompt child support payments that you earn by taking higher stress, larger responsibility, longer hours and commute, poorer working conditions, and more dangerous jobs necessary to make the payments. She has the right to protest your "unequal" pay in these jobs. You have the obligation of being killed softly in these jobs. She has the right to receive financial aid from the government. You have the obligation to go to war and perhaps be killed for the government. I trust that you see an element of unfairness in all this. It's no wonder that she lives, on average, seven years longer than you do.

The sixth way to survive women's liberation is to see the situation clearly for what it is.

Chapter Seven

WEARING THE PANTS

A guy was laying down the law, as he was laying down his new girlfriend. As she prepares for bed, he tosses her his pants and says, “Put these on.” She does, and they are much too big.

“I can’t wear these,” she says.

And he says, “That’s right, babe, and don’t forget who does wear the pants.”

With that, she throws him her panties and says, "Put these on."

He tries, and says, "Hell, I can't get into your pants."

She gets out of bed, turns on the TV, mutters something that combines an expletive with the terms "pig," "male," "chauvinism," and "attitude," and says, "You got that right."

Feminist thinking is central to our modern day society. Feminism clearly intends to upend the patriarchal (the man wears the pants) family, and replace it with something that is being defined as we go along. This has created much confusion as to the role of male and female in our society. But within the confusion, there are rules. One such rule is that she has equal rights to wear the pants, and is free to replace you with a vibrating device at her pleasure.

The rules of the game have changed over the past twenty-five years. You will lose badly if you don't understand how they have changed. See chapter twenty-five for a complete description of her rules. She may let you think that you are wearing the pants—usually until you have married her, bought her a house, and given her babies. And then, you are in for a major surprise and a hard lesson. You were wearing the pants, but unfortunately the pants began to bulge. She traded you in on the cute trainer at the fitness center. Her replacement decision is completely "no fault." This means that there need not be any rationale or morality associated with her decision. This is just one example of how you can lose badly.

The seventh way to survive women's liberation is to forget about wearing the pants. So what do you wear? I suggest that you try wearing a tan at the nudist colony or those cute robes at the local monastery, or turn the page.

Chapter Eight

Gym Shorts

Are you unsure of what to wear? I definitely do not suggest that you call in the nearest female for consultation on tie or sock color. I do suggest that you put on gym shorts, and go to the local fitness center.

As described in the last chapter, one reason for this is that she may recycle you for her personal trainer, if you don't.

A better reason is that this will keep you fit. The benefits of this are obvious. You get to feel better, and probably live longer. As centenarian George Burns once said, "If I knew that I was going to last this long, I would have taken better care of myself."

An even better reason for going to the gym is that there is usually a congregation of female hard-bodies in skimpy spandex suits. Especially if you are in "ringless mode," this is a most pleasurable experience. It keeps your mind off the no pain/no gain thing, and off your last argument. The "ringless mode" is defined as those periods of time that follow a fight with your mate that does not end in sex. If you want to get judgmental about a guy taking his ring off, what's worse: his "ringless mode" for a couple of days, or her nagging for a couple of weeks? You are not having an affair; you are simply expressing your feelings in a nonverbal way. With or without your ring, looking is not a crime, and the gym is a healthy and acceptable place to look.

Arguably the best reason to wear gym shorts is pizza, beer, and ice cream. If you get really good at working out, theoretically you can eat whatever you damn well please.

I don't know if this is a good reason, but the process of staying fit is also the eighth way to survive women's liberation. You are beginning to learn from this book that being with feminists can be aggravating and stressful. Playing racquetball or getting on an aerobic machine for forty-five minutes is a great way to release tension. Also, when she is being a royal pain, this is a generally accepted excuse for getting out of the house. The eighth way is: when in doubt, wear gym shorts!

Chapter Nine

A Man's Bond

This chapter isn't, unfortunately, about some new sexual restraining device or bonding with a buddy at the ol' ball game.

This chapter is about a man's word being his bond.

Just because women have a certain prerogative doesn't mean that it's right. There is a real danger that female fickleness puts us and society into a downward spiral. It goes like this: if it's okay for her to trash me, then it's okay for me to trash the next one. Have you ever seen a guy get dumped by his girlfriend then seek out whatever one-night stand he can find? It's the pain and bitterness acting out, and it's not good for the guy or the gal. It's the "two wrongs trying to make it feel better" thing.

What is the proper response to female fickleness? Be a man; keep your promises.

Some examples:

- If you end a date and tell her that you are going to call her, then call her. It doesn't need to be for another date. You can just call and check on her dog, or whatever.
- If you say that you'll be picking her up at six in the evening, then be there on time (or try like hell to get to a phone).
- If you tell her that you are going to earn money from your latest fly-by-night venture, or get a job by a certain date so you can marry her, then do it. This can be a job at the local McDonalds—it's still a job.
- If the child support check is "in the mail," then make damn sure that it's in the mail.
- And the big one: if you vow that you will love, honor, and cherish her until death, then honor the commitment.

A promise is a promise; an agreement is an agreement; a vow is a vow. It doesn't change just because something came up that made keeping it more difficult. It doesn't change just because you have a good lawyer who can get you out of it. It doesn't change because you now see that what you originally agreed to do was a dumb idea. This is a great way to show a female how to wear pants.

You get the idea. The concept is simple: a man's word is his bond.

C h a p t e r T e n

DIVORCE COURT

Love is blind. As men, we seem to have a bad habit of bumping into things.

Having been through a divorce, actually two divorces, I recommend that all men spend an hour in divorce court before they get married. You wouldn't make an investment without evaluating the risks, so why would you consider getting married without understanding the downside?

I had coffee this morning with a divorce attorney. I asked him what counsel he had for men in their approach to relationships. He didn't have any, which told me something. However, he did mention that his comment to incoming male clients is that the guy can expect to pay 60 percent of his future income for the ex-wife's alimony and child support. The client's typical reaction is to think about this for a moment, and say, "Hell, that's not so bad; 40 percent is more than I'm getting now!"

My impression is that most guys expect the worst as they approach divorce court. Their expectations are generally exceeded. It is a give-and-take divorce. You give; she takes.

You must remember that this is your divorce, not your lawyer's. You must gather all your strength and put aside the bitterness, pain, and anger. Try and then try again to work out a settlement directly with your wife, and hand it to your attorneys for documentation and implementation. If the lawyers get in control, you will see increasing levels of antagonism, and you will pay big time. The lawyers will win, and you and your soon-to-be ex-wife will lose.

Marriage and divorce are a bad—very bad—financial deal for most men. This is because men usually earn more than women, and the divorce seeks to split the assets acquired during the marriage equally. In other words, she will get all of hers, and a part of yours. In addition, if there are children, you'll pay for the kids and for her loss of skills while caring for them. She is liberated, and divorce is "no fault." She can therefore trigger this financial disaster at any time for any reason. Can you see why marriage might be a bad deal?

The tenth way to survive women's liberation is to make sure that the "court" in your courting doesn't refer to divorce.

How do most men and all bats make love? Blindly!

Chapter Eleven

Selection

How do you avoid relationship disasters and divorce? The most important thing that you can do is make absolutely sure that you mate with the right person. This is, win, lose, or draw, the most important bet (decision) that you will make in your lifetime. So how do you improve the odds?

Randy's Top Five Tips for Selecting a Mate:

NUMBER FIVE: Is she great in the sack? This is the consideration that tends to distort or close down thinking about the others. It certainly needs to be on the list, but it's dangerous as hell. Most women are good in bed. Why is it that we tend to believe that the one with whom we're currently having the orgasm is the best? This needs to be a qualifier or disqualifier, not the deal maker in the selection process.

NUMBER FOUR: Is she beautiful enough to sleep with for the rest of your life? And will she stay that way? This needs to be on the list, but it's almost as deceptive as number five. Have you ever walked into a room and been blinded by a pretty face or exceptional cleavage? Your speaking apparatus is about as nimble as the beef tongue that you might find in the meat case of the supermarket. What's the point of her sex appeal, if it's all show and no go? Selecting a woman for her beauty alone is like buying a book for its cover or a house for its paint.

NUMBER THREE: Is she employed, and will she stay employed? I kind of like the female attitude on this. That is, if you are going to pick one, you might as well pick a rich one. Since we are stuck with this liberation nonsense, we might as well take full advantage of her independence. The problem with placing this too high on the list is that career women, upon getting pregnant, morph into stay-at-home mothers.

NUMBER TWO: Do you have a similar vision of what your togetherness will be? Do you like to do the same things? You can't spend all of your time in bed. So now what? Well, it's a plus if you can agree on where to live, how many children you want and how often you'll have sex. It's also a plus if she can do more than babble and eat bonbons. The difficulty with getting involved as a result of similar vision and interests is that they usually change over time.

AND, NUMBER ONE: For the top tip in selecting a mate, turn to chapter twelve.

Chapter Twelve

Commitment and Compassion

YOUR CRITERIA
IS THIS WOMAN COMMITTED AND COMPASSIONATE?

HER CRITERIA
IS THIS THE MAN WITH WHOM I WANT MY CHILDREN SPENDING ALTERNATE WEEKENDS?

Randy's Top Five Tips for Selecting a Mate . . . continued:
AND, NUMBER ONE: Is she capable of commitment and compassion?

There is a sickness that has reached epidemic proportions among females today. I have met a lot of women in my dating travels over the past few years. They frequently have two things in common. One, they are liberated, and two, they have had a succession of relationships with guys, and there was something terribly wrong with each one of them. You know what that means; the poor bastards got dumped. She is now back in circulation, again looking for the perfect Mr. Right. So what's the point? If no guy has been right, you can be sure that you will be the next Mr. Wrong. It's just a matter of time. Looking for Mr. Right, finding him, and finding him to be Mr. Wrong are symptoms of a deadly virus that is often attached to liberation. You'll recall that she is liberated from you, friend. I am suggesting that you look carefully at her relationship history with this in mind. This can be a good way to evaluate how compassionate she is.

If she is unable to keep her commitments in the small things, she most certainly won't keep them in the big things. Does she keep dates? Is she on time? Does she do what she says she is going to do? The answers had better be "YES." If not, it's best to cut your losses and get out fast. The longer you stay, the more you will hurt when it ends. In this age of liberation, women seem to easily justify breaking their commitments. I am suggesting that you be sensitive to her propensity for mind changes, as it will help you assess her capacity for commitment to you.

Without commitment and compassion, she will eventually find your flaw, and off she will go. Your heart will be broken. Her commitment and compassion are more important in selecting a mate than all the other areas combined.

You have your selection criteria, and she has hers. Her evaluation of you may answer the question, "Is this the man with whom I want my children spending alternate weekends?"

P.S. Is your own level of commitment and compassion consistent with what you are expecting from your prospective mate?

Chapter Thirteen

DATING AND COURTSHIP

I saved the number thirteen for this subject. It's perfect, don't you think? A peacock peers into a glass building and discovers a peacock of indescribable beauty and color. He seizes the moment and yells to this stunning bird shimmering in the building, "Will you marry me? I will love and care for you forever."

The object of his affection, after some reflection, sheepishly replies, "Get real, you fool, you are looking at your reflection." Are we seeking ourselves reincarnated in the opposite sex? Dating requires that we encounter, and sometimes kiss, frogs, peacocks, and somewhat-human creatures.

Actually, the concept of dating is simple. It's a giant networking exercise with the purpose of applying your selection criteria to the available pool of females. Networking is just the process of being in the flow of meeting single females. The possibilities are limitless. There are friends, family, church groups, interest groups (golf, gourmet, travel, alumni, et cetera), the local coffee shop, the internet and dating services. I have nothing against bars, but there is something tacky about meeting a life mate there. Other than bars, I suggest that you try it all, because eventually SHE will appear.

You must remember what you are doing. I understand horny and lonely. I understand that there is an enormous vulnerability to satisfy this emptiness by getting laid. Try like hell to stay away from this because it will blind you to your selection criteria. You will be on your way to more, not less, heartache. You must remember that you are looking for qualities like commitment and compassion. You will hopefully have fun exploring mutual interests while you evaluate these deeper qualities.

The lovemaking should mean that you are making love. And this means that you are moving to a committed relationship. You have established a meaningful friendship, and can articulate a shared vision of your future together. I met this fellow at the coffee house yesterday who is hopelessly in love—I mean hopelessly. And his girlfriend is telling him that she wants to date other men. This poor guy was in major heartache. This is not an example of a shared vision. It shows why you need to have a selection criteria and take the time to use it. This might take something like six months of dating and evaluation—before sex. Or should it be six days of dating before a sexual evaluation? How long do you wait before having sex? Please see chapter forty-eight. How do peacocks make love? Colorfully.

Good luck; you'll need it.

Chapter Fourteen

Relationship

You can be in a committed, exclusive, monogamous, and sexual relationship without being married. I am suggesting that you live together for a while, preferably a long while, before you get married and start having children.

You have completed your thirteenth date and six months and one night together. You are somewhere in the stratosphere, between passionate love and glorious lust. You know that this is true love, because she will actually sleep in a tent, or ride a hog, or whatever other wild, kinky, and improbable activity that you may happen to enjoy. What's more, she thinks you are the most wonderful, romantic, sexy, handsome, and intelligent male since Zeus. And like Zeus, she knows that you can perform godlike feats. She knows this because she has seen you turn the ceiling into stars. This is real love, and so now what?

Well, you decide to live together in a committed, exclusive, monogamous relationship. I believe that this is for real; this is not a trial run. You have determined that you have a shared vision, as well as common values and interests. You are going for it; this relationship is forever. If you are not clearly to this place, don't waste your time living with this person. Continue dating.

But no, this is real love, and you decide to live together. This is where romantic love turns into a relationship, a twenty-four-hour-a-day, seven-day-a-week relationship. This is when you nurture your relationship skills, in preparation for the "M" word. There is a whole lot involved in relationship building. I describe these skills from a man's perspective later in the book. We need to take the time necessary to get this right. Most people think nothing of spending four or five months preparing for marriage. Looking at the divorce rate, this isn't working. In fact, it's an unmitigated disaster of heartbreak, legal fees, custody battles, and broken families. People spend four or five years getting prepared for a profession. Isn't a happy, lifelong relationship more important than a career? Is she in love with you, or with the idea of walking down the isle?

That is why I suggest that the fourteenth way to survive women's liberation is to take four or five years in relationship development before getting married and having children. In five years, you and your mate will have each earned a master's degree in relationship from the old School of Hard Knocks.

Chapter Fifteen

If You Really Loved Me . . .

Sometime between month six and month eighteen of the relationship, you will likely hear her mumble, "If you really loved me, you would marry me." Over time, the volume and pitch of this may increase until it becomes absolutely deafening. She may also become increasingly and silently resentful.

The fifteenth way to survive women's liberation is to be prepared for this. Your response is to tell her that you love her and are committed to her. And that you will marry her sometime prior to the end of the fifth year of your relationship, provided she doesn't exercise her prerogative during that time. You should remind her that this will require a prenuptial agreement that says that what is mine is mine, and what is yours is yours. Actually, this is a part of the vision that should be discussed during your courtship. Please see chapter seventeen.

Her problem with living together has nothing to do with the sincerity of your love. You love this woman, and she knows that you love her. You are showing it every day by living with her in a committed, exclusive, and monogamous relationship. So what's the problem? She has three problems. First, living with a man out of wedlock is not socially acceptable for her. Second, she wants you legally obligated to be sleeping with her and providing for her. Finally, marriage legitimizes her status as mother of your future children. Those are valid reasons for her. Again, please understand that her arguments for marriage have nothing to do with love.

Your problems with marriage relate mainly to the legal issues (please review chapter ten, which deals with divorce court). By getting married, you subject your assets, as well as your current and future earnings, to the mercy of the divorce court. Being liberated, she gets to trigger this nightmare at any time, for any reason. Your financial well-being is now vulnerable to her PMS and/or to the attentions of her trainer at the fitness center. These are some of the reasons why women make emotional (and poor) decisions, and why you should take your time getting into marriage. You want to make damn sure that she is completely committed to the relationship, and fully loyal to you. As her mumble of the "M" word becomes more shrill, you should become more cautious.

Is she more interested in marriage, babies, security, and money, or in loving you? Time will tell.

Chapter Sixteen

Will You Marry Me?

A wise man once was asked, "Do smart men make good husbands?" He replied, "Smart men don't get married."

You have now spent several years in a relationship. You know fully the meaning of morning breath and PMS. She understands that you are capable of a snort while asleep that makes the dog bark, and of a stubble that can sand sandpaper.

You have fought, cried, laughed, and had great sex. She thinks you're the best thing since chocolate. And you think she's the best thing since catching a two-hundred-pound marlin. I mean, this is serious, forever love.

Before you pop the question, I suggest that you go have a little chat with the father of the bride-to-be and let him know your intentions regarding his daughter. This shows a bit of class, particularly if she isn't pregnant. It also gives you the opportunity to discuss, man to man, the upcoming wedding plans. You should suggest that it would make enormous good sense for you and his daughter to elope. The reason for this is that it will preclude a lot of fuss and the money saved can be used on the down payment on a home, on his daughter's retirement account, or on a college fund for his grandchildren. He has to agree with your logic on this. This gives you a chance to see what kind of man he is, and if he has any clout in his household. The chances are that he has zero clout, but it's worth a try.

He gives permission. You actually remember the ring, and she says "yes." Oh hell, what have you done? You are engaged! Hope has triumphed over reason.

This is such a joyous time. Your mate is into major event planning—the flavor of the cake, the placement of the disc jockey, the pattern of silver—that type of stuff. This is important for her and especially for her mother, and she is busy, busy, busy. All you need to know about getting married is that her father is paying for it, she and her mother are arranging it, and you had best get the hell out of the way or you could get hurt.

For you, the engagement is about trip planning. I'm referring to two trips, the honeymoon and . . .

Chapter Seventeen

Prenuptials

. . . and the trip to your lawyer about the prenuptial agreement. You remember the agreement that you discussed with her during the courtship. You did remember to discuss this with her during the courtship, didn't you? It's the one that says what's yours is yours, and what's hers is hers.

Lawyers write books on this subject; you can pick one up at the library or bookstore. I am not an attorney, and do not wish to try practicing law here. But I will make a suggestion. If you have any future income worth keeping, or any separate property worth protecting, you should at least look into this. You may have nothing now, but twenty years from now, things could be different.

With advances in medicine, we are living longer. A lifetime can be a long time, a very long time, living with one person. Men get painted as the bad guy when they start chasing the young skirts. Condoning this sort of thing is not biblically or politically correct; however, moralizing about it gets complicated. When females bash a guy for having an affair with a younger woman, they never mention the underside of his primary relationship:

- the wife that constantly nagged him with her lists and rules.
- the wife that had an ongoing litany of excuses to avoid having sex with him.
- the wife that always expected more, regardless of what she received, and regularly let him know it.
- the wife that let herself go to seed, mentally and/or physically.

After ten, twenty, thirty, or forty years of this, the guy finally seeks comfort somewhere, and he ends up being the bad guy. Where do you draw the line between the pain of staying in the relationship and honoring your commitment to it? The answer can be gut wrenching (do I or don't I), guilt inducing (trash commitment and damage family), and life shortening (live with her abuse and with the pain). This is why men are fearful about marriage. This is why you should take four or five years to understand what you are getting before you marry her. And it's why you should consider a prenuptial agreement.

The husband finds his wife in bed with another man. The guy coolly confronts the disheveled couple. He asks, "Are you having a bad hair day or is it something else?"

"You see?" says the wife to her lover laying beside her. "Didn't I tell you he's stupid?" If she exercises her prerogative, you will be injured. But a prenuptial agreement will help to prevent her from adding insult (financial ruin) to the injury (relationship breakup).

Chapter Eighteen

The Ozzie and Harriet Trap

Yes, I realize that there are still traditional Ozzie and Harriet relationships. Today, they are called "powerpoint" relationships, with the female dependent on and expressing through her man. The husband goes to work, and the wife stays at home and cares for the children.

Some men see this traditional type of relationship as the highest expression of family values in our society. Some women like this arrangement because they get to stay at home and be Mom, the homemaker and American princess. Some guys may think that they have more control in this type of relationship, because they are making the money, and she is dependent on them.

However, the powerpoint relationship is a bad deal for the man. Ultimately, this control is an illusion, because she can always exercise her prerogative. Her ability to make a no-fault mind change gets to why this type of relationship is more dangerous for the male. When a dependent female changes her mind, you will be supporting a "helpless and unskilled" person, in the manner to which she has become accustomed. It is called "alimony," and possibly "child support." It's expensive, and it happens in many marriages.

Contrast this with the alternative of coupling with an independent woman who can support herself. If you have children in a divorce, you will lose time with them and gain the legal obligation to financially support them. But at least you won't be stuck for alimony. Think about it.

My parents had an Ozzie and Harriet relationship during most of their marriage, and it worked for them. I see examples, but only a few happy examples, of this type of marriage in our contemporary society. They are few because most women want to be liberated or independent. Still, these relationships can be wonderful. The guy gets to go out, slay dragons, and be the provider. The gal gets to stay home, and make and nurture children. I can understand why you may wish to try it. If you have considered the risks, and want to go for it—great! At least you have been forewarned.

Chapter Nineteen

Mary, Monique, Melody, and Melissa

You know who I am referring to here. Mary is the cute coed you met in college, with whom you spent Sunday afternoons at the beach. Monique, oh Monique, is the cute French waif you dated during that month in Paris on the training program. Melody is the lady you met while working down the hall at your former employer. And Melissa is the neighbor with whom you teamed up on the symphony fundraiser. You have known these people for years (has it been that long?). They are dear to you, and you love each in a special way. They are your women friends.

These friendships may or may not have begun with a romantic interest or involvement. Over the years, however, each friendship has evolved and weathered to the point of being comfortable. She has gotten married and had children and lived life. She has seen you through your dating and relationship and marital escapades. You know she will continue to be there. And you know she will be real. You may see or talk to her once a year or once a month. It doesn't matter, because when you talk to her it's like you last saw her yesterday. There may be gaps in time, but there are no gaps in caring or concern. The friendship is seamless.

You have told your mate about Mary, Monique, Melody, and Melissa. Let's face it, this can be touchy. If your mate is insecure, this can be very touchy. You have nothing to hide; you are not sleeping with these women. I suggest that you definitely reveal them, and preferably introduce them to your mate. Since Monique is still in Paris and Melody is now in New York, this can be difficult. Do the best you can.

Your women friends are very important. If and when your mate does a mind change, your female friends will be there. You can rely on them for a female perspective that will give you a reality check on whatever craziness is going on in your life. A man can confide in a woman friend what he cannot reveal to a mate. If love is blind, friendship closes its eyes.

The nineteenth way to survive women's liberation is to keep and nurture your women friends.

Chapter Twenty

Keep Your Head Down

What should you do when she goes into one of her female down-cycles? There are four things to do.

First, understand that women do suffer. It's called "Premenstrual Syndrome" (PMS), "During Menstruation Syndrome" (DMS), and other emotional stuff that can cause them to go into severe tailspins. You must be able to see when this is happening. Recognizing it is not difficult. Most men have a keen, well-developed, intuitive feel for it. Is she acting like a bitch?

Second, if you unwittingly get caught in the line of fire, I strongly suggest that you move into rapid retreat. This means that you should get out of the way as quickly and as gracefully as possible. You should not attempt to argue with her. You most certainly should not attempt to reason with her. You will not win. And you will only make matters worse.

Third, the best place to deal with a female down-cycle is in your foxhole. I suggest that you dig it deep, and that you be very careful about coming out. This will protect you from her small-arms fire, but you are still vulnerable to her artillery.

Fourth, since you are hiding out, this is sure to piss her off even more. She wants to do battle. Keep your damn head down.

All good men have spent time there. Good luck, friend.

P.S. What's the difference between a female with PMS/DMS and a pitbull? Lipstick.

Chapter Twenty-One

SEASONS

WHY ARE HURRICANES GIVEN FEMALE NAMES?

The seasons teach us many things. There is a wonderful cycle in nature that governs all living beings, both literally and figuratively.

WINTER

The nights are longest, darkest, and coldest in winter. This gives us time for rest and reflection. We need time to stop and get in touch with ourselves. It is time to put in perspective our mandate from culture, mate, boss, and especially ego to "be a man" and "win." Winter can be difficult, because we can get lost in the darkness of searching for ourselves. The trees are bare. It is a time to remember that they will bear fruit again and that spring is just around the corner.

SPRING

This is a time for planting, birth, and rebirth. If you have ever seen a wildflower bloom or a baby born, you will understand spring in the deepest way possible. This is the time that we move from reflection to a dream to a goal. We begin to see more light shine on our pathway, and we want to be moving along. This is the time for practicing patience and for being content with our place on the journey. The blessings of spring are many; it's new, fresh, exciting, and revealing.

SUMMER

Have you ever seen the fields of corn or wheat being caressed by a breeze on a long, hot, August day? The planning and planting are beginning to pay off. This is a time that we may take a snapshot of the rows upon rows of crops, and forget that growth is actually taking place. Nurturing can be hard work, and it is very much man's work. We are beginning to see the fruits of our labor.

FALL

It is harvest time. We enjoy the bounty. We see the vibrant colors and feel the invigorating crispness of the autumn. We celebrate the culmination of our seasonal journey with our loved ones and friends. And the cycle repeats . . .

As a man, you can celebrate the special blessings of each passing season. Or relax; if you don't care for today's weather, it will soon change. Finding fulfillment in the joys of the season can bring you to your rightful place of earth father, husbandman of our surroundings. This is the twenty-first way to survive.

P.S. Why are hurricanes given female names? When they come they're wild and wet, but when they go they take your house and car with them.

Chapter Twenty-Two

"Men Are Cheap"

A psychologist friend revealed to me that the single biggest complaint of her female clients and friends is that "men are cheap." Does this sound familiar?

You are once again in a no-win situation with this one. If you agree, you are guilty as accused. If you disagree, they have you right where they want you. This proves that you have a seemingly unlimited line of credit with your American depressed card. She doesn't expect much, just a nice dinner out once a week at a restaurant of her choice, then the theater tickets, then the cruise, and so on. This is how high she wants you to jump, Mr. Prince Charming.

There is a major problem with man in the role of generous provider as we move into the new millennium with liberation. You have allowed a situation in which you are spending your money and she is saving her money. When you are poor, she will be heading for the door. At some point in the future, she has the wealth and you have the life experience. There is something wrong with this picture. I hope you see it earlier, rather than later. Don't get flattered into the generosity trap.

There is another problem with the position of generous provider. By assuming the status of Mr. Prince Charming, you further the helpless and unskilled princess syndrome. You are now subject to paying alimony, and you may pay big. You will have none of the benefits of female companionship, and all of the expenses. This is not a good deal, so don't set yourself up for it in the first place.

The answer to this no-win situation is to admit that yes, you *are* cheap. I like this approach because it's direct, and disarming. It also quickly weeds out the ladies that are simply looking for a meal ticket. Another approach is to try elevating the discussion to living simply. (Please see chapter forty-five.) Since most people do not live with this philosophy in our society, your chances of winning with this are slim. Fairness may have to suffice.

I have a theory that guys who attempt to buy women's respect have a low self image. They feel like they must pursue, perform, and pay in order to qualify for her love. The lower the guys' self esteem, the more they need to give. You can't buy love.

She is making her own money, and she can damn well share expenses with you.

Chapter Twenty-Three

The Golden Rule

HE OR SHE
WHO HAS THE GOLD
MAKES THE RULES

THE GOLDEN RULE

Her attitude about money will reveal much about how she feels—about herself and about you. Respect for money is connected with respect for who is providing it, including herself. Unhappiness with herself or hostility toward you can drive a woman to orgies of spending; it is a way of inflicting self destruction or punishment.

Listed below are various ways to share expenses with her. We are dealing with money here. Caution: this may be emotional.

1) You are dating and you alternate paying for dates with her. You can try to justify this based on fairness. Stay away from the idea that if she pays she won't need to feel obligated to have sex with you. This will backfire on you, since it links the payment of money with sex. If you pay, she's a whore. If you don't pay, you're cheap. She may try the "if you really loved me, you would pay" trap. Remember, this is about the fairness of sharing expenses.

2) You are in a real living-together relationship. You keep your income in your account, and you pay your bills. She keeps her income in her account, and she pays her bills. And you both agree to divide the joint bills and pay them individually. And/or you both agree to fund a kitty to pay for common expenses.

When you are deciding who pays what, it may be helpful to keep in mind that women have a tendency to forget the Golden Rule. You know, the rule that says, "He or she who has the gold makes the rules." If you pay for something, that means that you have control over what happens with that something. If your mate has more money than you, the same rule applies. Beware of the overly generous female who buys you for a price. The price will be that you do exactly as she wishes.

3) You comingle your revenues, and she pays the bills. Women like this arrangement the best, because you usually make more money and she typically spends more money. She gets to spend hers and spend yours. A friend was telling me recently about this couple that comingles. The husband got a thirty-thousand-dollar year-end bonus. Within three months, the wife was trying to figure out how and where she spent it. There are certain pitfalls with the comingle approach that are obviously dangerous for men. I don't recommend this alternative.

4) You keep your money and pay all bills, including an allowance to your mate. This is a classic powerpoint situation. If this sounds good, please review chapter eighteen. Remember the benefits of "MEN ARE CHEAP."

Chapter Twenty-Four

UNDERSTANDING WOMEN

This is an oxymoron. Women don't understand women. What makes you think you can? If you try to understand her, you will suffer the same fate as trying to follow her rules, as described in the next chapter.

Women should have been delivered with directions. We are supposed to just know if, when, and how to fondle, kiss, rub, suck, lick, or blow dry. Finding the proper receptacle comes naturally enough, but this other stuff requires instructions. The trouble is that even if we men were given such directions, we wouldn't take the time to actually read them. I have come to the profound belief that God is masculine, and He had responsibility for creating woman. When He got done with the assembly (having refused to read the instructions), He found a loose screw and two washers at the bottom of the shipping crate. He created a woman that is obviously operable, but one wonders about the loose screw. As my friend Bubba observed, "even if we were to understand women, we wouldn't believe it."

It is a far better use of your limited time and energy to understand yourself.

P.S. In the beginning God created Earth and rested. Then God created man and rested. Then God created woman. Since then, neither God nor man has rested.

Chapter Twenty-Five

Her Rules

The female is the keeper of the rules. The male is not competent to understand any of the rules. Any male who presumes to know any rule will be banished to a place of sexual limbo.

The female and her rules are always correct. If the female is not right, it is due to the male's malfunction or ignorance.

The male must always act with proper contrition and guilt for his continual malfunction and ignorance.

The female has a special prerogative that gives her the right of mind change at any time. Her rules may be changed without warning. Also, the female may say whatever she wants to say, whenever she wants to say it—and then retract it. The male may only reconsider something if the male gives the female proper notice of his intent to reconsider, and if the female gives him the right to reconsider.

The female may be mad and throw stuff if she pleases. The male must be peaceful and accommodating at all times. The female may provoke the male to anger. Having done so, the female will condemn the male as "abusive, unstable, and neurotic" for expressing his feelings.

The female may have friends, but any interest by the male in having female friends is "womanizing," and in having male friends is "homosexual."

The male must be fully qualified in extra sensory perception and lip reading so as to know what he needs to know about the intentions of the female.

The female must always keep the male guilt-ridden and on the defensive. If the male expresses his strength, he is "aggressive." If the male shares his feelings, he is a "sissy." If the male exercises leadership, he is "domineering" and "controlling." If the male is an able provider and successful, he is a "workaholic." If the male enjoys cuddling and other forms of physical expression, he is "oversexed."

The female will be ready for whatever she is ready for whenever she is ready for it. The male must always be ready.

Any publication, reproduction, or dissemination of the rules by a male is punishable by physical and/or financial castration. The male who doesn't accept her rules is "inflexible" and a poor excuse for a man.

Please understand that she actually believes that these are the rules. This is okay; let her believe it. However, if you follow her rules, you will either go nuts or die early. The twenty-fifth way to survive women's liberation is to live by your own rules.

Chapter Twenty-Six

We Need To Talk

For most men, these are some of the most frightening words in the English language. If it's simply "We need to talk," you are in deep you-know-what, and you're about to do time in your foxhole.

If you are lucky, it's "Darling, we need to talk." This type of talk is actually about communication. This isn't fighting.

This isn't play time. This isn't screwing around. We are referring to real sit-down-and-work-something-out communication here.

This is important. As a single person, we could just do it. As soon as we enter a relationship, everything is up for discussion. This includes the texture of the toilet paper, the scent of the shampoo, the firmness of the mattress, and the method of squeezing the toothpaste tube.

This is serious, because if you can't talk and work it out, your relationship probably won't survive. This will eventually be true regardless of how good the sex is. So *we* need to learn how to do this. (I say "we" because one-person communication usually doesn't work well.)

There are five possible outcomes to the communication process.

First, we talk for the pure pleasure of talking. This is more of a girl thing, but it can be entertaining for guys, too.

Second, we agree to agree. This is the best result, and the most difficult to achieve. If men and women agree, their way of getting there is always different.

Third, we compromise. This is where we try to get to the "win/win" place that normally is achieved only in books on communication. In real life, it's usually a "this person loses this and that person loses that" deal. So the trick is to find joy in whatever is the area of agreement. Six nights a week of great sex isn't half bad.

Fourth, we compartmentalize. This gives us the opportunity to agree to do it her way *and* his way. She goes to Aspen; you go to Tahiti.

Fifth, we agree to disagree. This is related to the one above. It is an acceptable outcome, since we agree. She has her rules, and you have THE GOLDEN RULE.

Hopefully, everyone is reasonably pleased, if not happy, with the outcome. More important than the outcome, however, is the feeling that you had an opportunity to fully express and be heard in the communication process.

There is one secret for a man communicating with a female. She will go along with you if you know where you're going, and if you just shut up and listen to her while you're going there.

Chapter Twenty-Seven

EQUAL RIGHTS

Most women have joined the feminist fight for equal rights. Gloria and her troopers know exactly what they are fighting. It's that terrible glass ceiling. These women want to be taken seriously and treated with respect. As good red-blooded American men, we need to do the right thing: take up those burning bras and join the crusade for equal rights.

I, for one, would like to look up to more women through that glass ceiling. If women are so offended by our looking at their legs, why do they wear those cute short skirts? Although not related to the glass ceiling issue, the same is true of cleavage. Somehow we are supposed to notice and not notice at the same time. This takes practice. Those mirrored sunglasses are helpful for this, but somewhat obvious when used to observe the ceiling. I look forward to the day women get their equal right to walk on glass.

"My wife is a fool to want equal rights," said this guy to his buddy. "She would be constantly bitching with so few." The problem with equal rights is that the rights are not equal—for men. A prime example: if a female earns it, she gets to spend it. Unfortunately, it doesn't always work so well the other way. If a man earns it, she expects to spend or decide how to spend it.

Here is an example of how this *should* work. You pay for the mortgage, insurance, taxes, and utilities on your home. She brings her clothes. You are such a sweet, generous man for paying the bills. And since you pay the bills, you get to say what goes on with the damn house. The rules are: she pays for it; she controls it; he pays for it; he controls it. That's equal rights. "Equal rights" does not mean "special rights."

Did you hear about the executive director of a major feminist organization who concluded her pro-ERA speech with a plea to the members? She pounded the lectern and said, "As long as women are split like we are, men will remain on top."

P.S. Comparable pay for comparable work? Absolutely!

Chapter Twenty-Eight

IN THE FLOW

$E=MC^2$. Based on this relationship, there is a constant flow and virtually unlimited store of energy within the universe. To live life fully, we need to understand and work with this flow. The chemical composition of water is H_2O. "H" stands for hydrogen. Have you seen what happens when you split a hydrogen atom in a certain way? "O" stands for oxygen. Have you seen what happens when you burn liquid oxygen in a rocket engine? There is no shortage of energy in the universe. Our challenge is to be in alignment with its flow.

Life is like a raindrop. If we keep adding raindrop on raindrop of thoughtful energy (preferably positive), soon we have created something significant. A few drops of constructive thinking a day add up to a powerful river of life.

Life is like being in a boat on a river. We will get further if we are willing to get in the current. We don't want to be stuck on the shore, or to fight our way upstream. Navigating it can be exciting and hazardous, with its rapids and debris.

Life is like being a paddle wheel on a river. The current of the river will generate energy for us, if we are open to it. If the river floods, the stuck wheel can actually be destroyed. Like the paddle wheel, we want to be working in harmony with life's energy flow.

Life is like a dam on a river. The dam will not function properly unless it is open to release. If the dam is closed to giving, eventually it will overflow and cease to function as a dam. Life's energy will flow into us, if we are open to giving.

Can you see how you can create and use the flow of energy in life?

P.S. If the river's current dumps your boat into the ocean, you will want to find a new energy to move you, like a sail. On second thought, I suggest you call your travel agent and book a cruise. You have earned it!

Chapter Twenty-Nine

Her New Boyfriend

SUGGESTED TRANSMITTAL:

DEAR TURKEY HEAD,

CONGRATULATIONS!

SINCE YOU WILL NEED MORE THAN BEST WISHES, I'M SENDING YOU *THE MAN'S BOOK*.

ALL MEN ARE IN THIS TOGETHER.

GOOD LUCK,

Former Turkey Head

She sends you the courtesy letter telling you about her new fiancé, the wonderful Mr. Right. As an aside, I just looked up "fiancé" in the dictionary. Did you know that my pocket dictionary has it located directly above "fiasco?" It's true. Anyway, she has a new boyfriend. So what to do?

You have discovered that she is not a goddess. She has exercised her prerogative; you can take solace in being set free from her nonsense. Your relationship with her developed to the point that you found each other's issues. She failed to see that this is where growth occurs. You can be comforted in the knowledge that she is soon to find a new and different (not better, just different) set of issues with this next guy.

Please understand that the poor bastard still has no clue as to her fickleness, and the shadows of her dark side are still a well-concealed mystery to him. He is probably in the mirage of "sweetness and spice and everything nice." He has no concept of Randy's top tip for selecting a mate, the loyalty issue. If she wasn't loyal to you, can she be expected to be loyal to him?

He is just some nice, unsuspecting guy, trying to do the best he can. So give him the benefit of the doubt.

Do something positive for your fellow man. Get his address, and send him a copy of this book A.S.A.P. He might learn something. His reaction to what he learns will be good for her, in the same way that a man's enrolling in a canine training school is good for his dog. And this will make you feel much better. Contrary to popular opinion, living well is not the best revenge. Getting even is the best revenge. I admit it; my revenge was writing this book. Your revenge can be sharing it with him. My hope is that this "revenge" comes from love. All men are in this together. Perhaps if we avoid the worship of goddess and the service of princess, we, together, will find a better, happier place.

The man who loves well will forget; the man who forgives all loves best.

Chapter Thirty

WOMAN BITES MAN

THE MAN'S BOOK, AKA
101 WAYS TO AVOID
SMACKING HER

The newspaper has a story today about a woman who has an abusive, controlling husband. He held her prisoner in their apartment. To make matters worse, the poor thing did not have a credit card or a car. Finally, she had enough. When her husband refused to let her drive his new car, they struggled over the keys and she bit him on the arm. The police came, looked at the bite mark, and arrested the wife.

And then there was the story about the female who hacked off the man's rather private and important body part while he was sleeping.

And there was the case of the woman who told police to take her husband or she would kill him. They talked to her and tried to calm her down. After they left, she beat him to death.

This kind of thing can be hazardous to your health. If you are being physically abused in a relationship, get help now. You may want to get some counseling. Your self esteem needs to get to a level beyond taking it like a man and selecting this type of woman in the future.

Spousal abuse is a human condition. Many two-sex studies have shown that men and women are equally likely to abuse. It isn't exclusively a problem of male as abuser. It just seems to be that way, because 90 percent of the police reports are made by women. Could it be that men are socialized to be ashamed to admit being abused by a female? The sad aspect of this is that the abuser has often been the victim of abuse at some prior time in his or her life.

There is a tendency in our legal system for a mandatory arrest if there is an injury in a spousal abuse situation. She is most certainly not worth going to jail for. If you have hit her, get help. There is nothing, *nothing* that she could have done to deserve being hit. There are therapists and male batterer support groups that can help you. There are at least a hundred and one ways to deal with her nonsense besides smacking her. Again, get help.

And then there is revenge using deception, trickery, and the LAPD. In Los Angeles, a man born with a bump on his head got his wife arrested three times for "abuse" before the police got wise. Good creativity and poor judgment—there are better ways to survive women's liberation.

Chapter Thirty-One

ABC's of Lust

Monogamous. Monogamous. Monogamous. After a while, it begins to sound like "monotonous." Orgasm. Orgasm. Orgasm. After a while, it begins to sound pretty good. The best reason for monogamy is that you will get more at home than on the road. She is your ticket to the stars. You are her ticket to the moon. She is there. You are there. Read the books and find a thousand and one ways to do it, and do them. If you are good at lovemaking, get better. This is the most pleasing, renewable resource on Earth, and it's free! It's theoretically "free," like a free lunch.

Sex with someone other than your mate is sinful, harmful, and hazardous. The Bible calls it "adultery." When (not if) your mate finds out, everyone involved will be hurt. You risk getting a sexually transmitted disease. These are the other reasons for faithfulness.

Express your lust constructively with women other than your mate. Visually undress the cute, young hard-body at the health club. Meet Mary for coffee. By all means enjoy lunch with Melody. Give Melissa a call. Send a letter to Monique in Paris. You will recall Mary, Melody, Melissa, and Monique from chapter nineteen. This will give you an outlet for female companionship and some diversity in your life. We are real men living in the real world; most of us are not monks.

But stay out of the hotel room with them, and for God's sake stay out of bed with them. Why? Let's summarize the reasons:

You will get some dreaded disease. Luck will carry you only so far. If you keep exposing yourself to the risk, eventually you will get nailed. It's called AIDS, herpes, et cetera. Please see chapter forty-eight.

Your mate *will* find out. Your mate has an intuitive sense about this kind of thing. She can smell the scent of another woman on you from the next room. She knows. Your mistress, regardless of what she tells you, has a vested interest in making sure that she knows. Your mate will find out.

It's more trouble than it's worth. The affair may begin as just great recreational sex. It never stays that way. The attraction may not be fatal, but it will be fatalistic. Sooner or later, your mistress will pull in the reins of entanglement.

You will get more at home. That is, unless you don't get more at home. There should be some advantages to her being geographically desirable. However, desirability may not translate into accessibility. Do you know how to keep an American princess from having sex? Marry her. If you don't get more at home, please see chapters sixty-six and sixty-seven.

Chapter Thirty-Two

When All Else Fails . . .

. . . it's time to see the therapist. Every relationship needs to designate a head shrink after the sheets cool down, with the following understanding: if our relationship gets into trouble, we will go see Philip, the psychologist. Either party may initiate two or three sessions with Philip, on demand, for any reason.

The trick is to reach this understanding when everything is wonderful. This is when you cannot possibly imagine that sweetness and spice could ever make you crazy. If things are not so great with the relationship, you will have a hard time agreeing on what to do and who to see. This agreement gives you a chance to trigger a visit with Philip before getting turned off completely. A therapy session is a whole lot cheaper than a consultation with a divorce attorney.

However a guy entering therapy needs to be careful that the sessions are fair, purposeful and effective. Members of the psychology profession completed a study to determine what keeps a marriage together. They found that "active listening" and "validation" were not effective. These are techniques commonly used by therapists to counsel couples. So what did work? The relationships that worked, according to the study, had one thing in common—the husband was willing to give in to his wife. Most guys intuitively know this, but we now have it in a published report based on a six-year study involving 130 couples. The implications are nauseating to me. The message for men is a simple choice: lose your wife or lose your balls. The feminists and libbers have men on the ropes backed into a very unhealthy corner. Perhaps we need to challenge Peter, the therapist, to find a more balanced way, that's not necessarily her way. Please see chapter 92, Getting to We, in this context.

There needs to be a limited number of sessions (perhaps three), to ensure that this is problem solving, not an exercise in full employment for the therapist. There needs to be an agreement that you are doing this to make the relationship work better. In other words, both people should be committed to the relationship, and to making the sessions productive. If only one person is serious, why waste your time? This process of confronting problems can be painful. But it will likely be much less painful than a gut-wrenching, tear-jerking breakup.

Hopefully, your relationship helper will get you to see the problem(s) from a different perspective and to move things off dead center. Sometimes we just get stuck in a recycling dynamic, constantly repeating a discussion of the same old issues. We need a magical breakthrough. It is tragic if you trash an otherwise perfectly good relationship for lack of getting a little help at the right time. If it doesn't work, at least you tried. Even if you decide to split, perhaps the sessions have helped you to do so as friends, with a somewhat friendly settlement and parting.

How do two ants screw in a light bulb? I don't know; I've never seen ants manage to get in a light bulb. Sometimes humans are like ants trying to find a way to screw in a light bulb, and they need somebody to turn them on to a little illumination.

Chapter Thirty-Three

Pregnancy and Murphy's Law

You know about the birds and bees. Now let me tell you about the facts of life. When it comes to women and getting pregnant, if it can go wrong, it will go wrong.

If you are not prepared to deal with a baby, keep it in your pants. Judging from the number of teenage pregnancies, this could stand repeating. Perhaps we need an advertisement in a men's magazine with a caption saying, "If you don't want one, don't do it—think responsible sex." This covers a picture of a guy changing a diaper that is graphically full of mush.

There is no such thing as birth control for the male. Condoms break and they slip off. The pill and other female forms of birth control are 99 percent effective *in the laboratory*. Why does that 1 percent always seem to pop up in real life? She may tell you that she is using a form of birth control and then "forget" to use it.

Birth control means that the female has a measure of control. From a male perspective, please understand that after you put it in, you have absolutely no control over what will happen next.

"I am pregnant." Next to "I love you," these are the three most emotional words in any language. What are you going to do when she calls to let you know that WE (she and you) are going to have a baby? It happens. It happens a lot. The answer is that you are going along for the ride. Trust me, you are not driving. If she is pro-choice, you may get one result. If she is pro-life, you may get another result. Child support, abortion, or adoption are possible results. She has the right to choose; you have the obligation to pay.

Men initiate sex and women receive. Women's receptivity seems to fulfill their biological imperative to create babies. As we initiate, we need to be responsible about the broader implications of what we are doing. There is more to this than getting another notch on our gun. The human species has become too successful for its own good, and we are creating babies at a pace that is beyond the capacity of the earth's resources to support and sustain the population. Mankind needs more love, more love-making, and fewer babies. This a way to guarantee that one or two children per couple are enough already. After you have had as many children as you wish, get a vasectomy. You will trade one or two days of discomfort for peace of mind. Then, you and Murphy (who said, "If it can go wrong, it will go wrong") and pregnancy can part company.

Sex is not fun and games. Sooner or later, you will get caught in the act. Think about it.

Chapter Thirty-Four

SEXUAL HARASSMENT

Sexual harassment is a big deal for women in the workplace. It's an even bigger deal for the female lawyers getting big fees for making this an even bigger deal.

So the thirty-fourth way to survive women's liberation is for you to avoid all forms of sexual harassment.

This is serious business that can adversely affect your career path and legal well-being. As such, you need to clearly understand the rules on sexual harassment in the workplace:

- Thou shalt not pinch or make advances.
- Thou shalt not make love on the office furniture if thou art her boss, since she can later claim that the mutual consent was really harassment.
- Thou shalt not tell off-color or suggestive jokes.
- Thou shalt not open any magazine showing naked ladies (excuse me, women's fashion magazines showing naked women are okay).
- Thou shalt not look at a female worker the wrong way, in her opinion.
- Thou shalt not comment about a female worker's body parts.
- Thou shalt not do anything that thou wishest not to be exposed in an open hearing of the United States Senate on CNN.
- Thou shalt not . . .

If you do this stuff in a manner that pleases her, it is okay. If she doesn't like it, she gets to file a harassment lawsuit. The law makes no exception for your intention. If it is her word against yours, her "bare assertion" of harassment will prevail without factual support. There is no equality under the law for men in this area. It protects the female who is provocative. It protects the female who uses her sexuality for an "unearned" advancement. It presumes that the man is guilty as accused of harassment, unless proven innocent.

Doesn't there seem to be a rather unappealing double standard here? I spend hours defining my aging body parts in the gym. I would love to have some tall, beautiful blonde come up to me in the workplace and suggestively admire my pecs and glutes. This would make my day. Am I alone here?

Come on ladies, lighten up.

Chapter Thirty-Five

Bob, Bill, Bo, and Bubba

She finally has you right where she wants you—in the Venus Guy Trap. (For a definition of the Venus Guy Trap, please see chapter sixty-six.)

You really are morally or legally obligated to sleep with her. You are trying to figure out how this affects the various areas of your life.

One of the adjustments is to see how your male buddies fit into the relationship picture. The nature of your friendships will invariably change. You and your rat pack won't or shouldn't be making the rounds of your old singles haunts of your dating days. The focus of discussion with your close male friends might even elevate to something beyond getting laid, like complaining about not getting laid.

There may be a tendency to emotionally collapse around your woman. She, her friends, and her family can easily become the new center of your universe. This is a bad thing, because you lose your life.

It's important that you retain your male friends for several reasons.

They give you an outlet for expression of interests that she just doesn't share. You know, the guy stuff: your tennis, basketball, hockey, or softball game.

They will support you when she gets female nuts, the DMS and PMS times. They will give you a sense of perspective on her female point of view, and keep you from getting (you know) whipped. When she exercises her prerogative, your male friends will be there for you with a beer and a crying towel.

They will give you something to counterbalance her female friends. It's your softball game on the night of her women's club. When she quotes Mary's view to support her contention, you can quote your friend, Bubba, to support your opinion, and so on. We're talking about bringing in expert witnesses to resolve the toothpaste-tube issue and other real-life problems.

The thirty-fifth way to survive women's liberation is to keep and nurture your male friends.

Chapter Thirty-Six

VISION

The man should be a leader in the relationship. One way to do this is to elevate your mate's thinking to a vision of what you can be as a couple. This involves moving the conversation to what you have together—the commonality/connection. What are the values, beliefs, and interests that you share?

These are the areas that define your relationship, or that should define your relationship.

Many couples allow issues like how the toothpaste tube gets squeezed to define their attitude about each other. For a description of her tendency to nag, please see chapter ninety-one. Can we please move beyond petty differences?

Consider your areas of agreement with respect to values, beliefs, and interests? Here are a few examples of each:

VALUES

Is our word our bond? Do we honor our commitments? Are we geared to similar attitudes about saving and spending money? Do we want our time together to be special? These are examples of certain values that we may share with our mate. If we share core values, they will tend to be the cement that binds us together in the relationship. So try to get the discussion focused on something meaningful and positive.

BELIEFS

Do we believe that a loving and gentle attitude can make a difference? Do we agree that sex is better than ice cream? Are we convinced that we need a date night once a week? Let's see if we can fully explore the range of beliefs that we share. Maybe we can broaden and deepen those common beliefs over time, and rejoice in what we have together.

INTERESTS

Do you see the relationship as a two-person team playing the game of life? Can we agree on a time for boy's night out and on a time for her evening with the quilting group? Do we love to discover those cozy little ethnic restaurants? The sharing of these times together creates a history of experiences that binds and enriches the relationship over time. The fun of it is to expand on and nurture what is working.

Maybe you could sit down with her and talk about one or two of the values, beliefs, and/or interests that you share. Write them down. The challenge is to be creative and look for new ways to illuminate the vision. Some couples ask "why?" Others ask "why not?"

Chapter Thirty-Seven

The Nature of Things

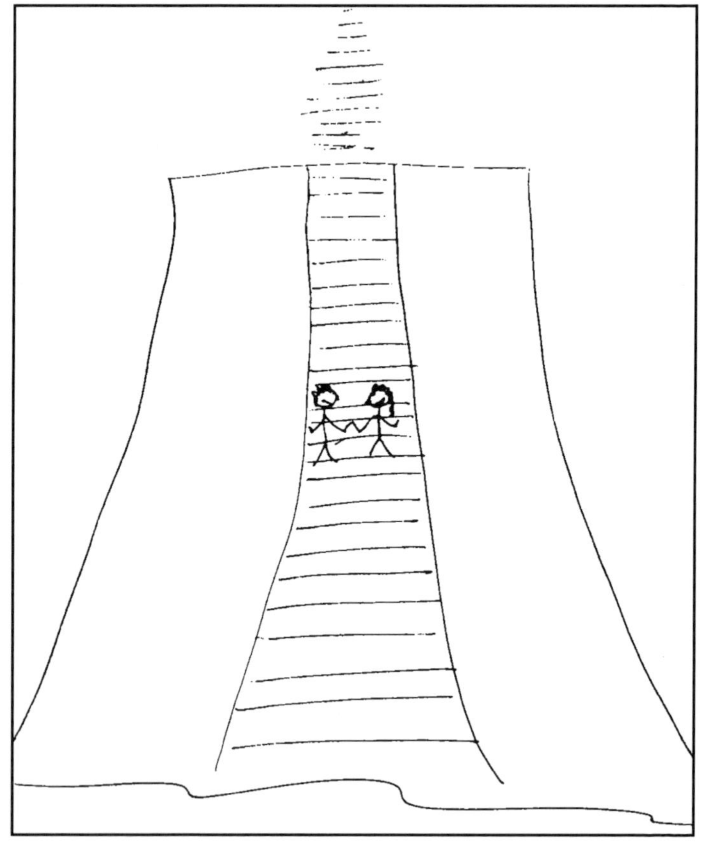

What's really happening here with this man/woman thing? This dance has been going on since Adam and Eve. It is an evolutionary biological imperative that is acted out on a daily basis. The woman is the gatekeeper who protects the mixture of genes to advance the evolution of humanity and civilization. ("If you want your sperm to enter my egg, you had better be strong and good.") This is a natural selection process that works to advance the species. It worked fairly well to get us to this level. At least we evolved beyond the ape and now have love affairs via FAX and e-mail.

As men, I think that we need to take a little more responsibility in this process. We seem to be moving around ready to pollinate whatever flower happens to be open, whenever it happens to be open. Life is not a game played with a male code calculated to score maximum sex with minimum commitment. We can do better than this.

This goes back to the selection process. We need to be sensitive to a woman's sense of commitment and compassion. Will she be loyal and forgiving? If her mind changes every six months or six years, you may well become the next dumpee. If her father was a jerk, and each of her last six boyfriends and/or husbands were jerks, guess what? You have found a scrotum-crunching bitch in search of her next victim. If you pollinate her flower, you soon will be in a Venus Guy Trap of emotional and financial hurt. If we, as men, took a little more care on the front end of the selection process, we could avoid this.

This has larger implications than our ability to avoid short-term pain. What kind of world would we have if people actually lived up to their commitments? What kind of world would we have if people actually were able to accept and forgive one another, and live in peace?

The nature of things is that we are moving up an evolutionary pathway. If we change the fundamentals of our human selection process at the mating level, the behavior patterns of the entire species will eventually evolve to a more loving, honorable place. What are we trying to do here?

Chapter Thirty-Eight

Love Letters

Females have a stereotype that men can't express their feelings. This is a bad rap. For example, if a guy is watching a football game and feels like getting a beer, it's no problem. He gives expression to that feeling by saying, "I feel like a beer." He then gets up, and gets the damn beer. Men are good at this touchy-feely stuff.

Sometimes, however, we just go along getting beers and forget that she is just back from stocking the refrigerator. You know someone actually brewed the beer, and someone actually carted the case from the store.

This is where love letters come in. You get a post-it (you know, those little stick-on things). You get a pen and you write something. Most anything will do. It can be something creative like, "Thanks for getting the beer; I love you." You don't want to start off too expressive, because she may not trust that this is actually happening. It may be preferable to misspell a word or two, so that she knows that this is real and didn't come from the gardener or something. What you say is not important. What's important is that you write something. She will like that. And she may bring you some chips and dip to go with the beer.

This also works when you are stuck in one of her down cycles. You just can't seem to talk to her. She is mad. You are mad. And the dog is hiding in the corner. What's nice about these little post-it things is that they come in packets of three zillion, and they are cheap. You might want to try something creative, like, "I'm sorry; I love U." This is the sort of random act of kindness that helps to break the ice.

You can put one on her pillow: "I think you're beautiful." You can hide one in her lunch bag: "I'm crazy in lust with you; get home soon." You get the idea. And if this gets you started, you might even get brave and try to link together a paragraph or a poem. Something endearing like:

"Roses are red
Violets are blue
You're the greatest
I love you."

Okay, I know—so what if we don't win the Nobel Prize for literature. At least we tried. The thirty-eighth way to survive women's liberation is to write a love letter.

Chapter Thirty-Nine

THE DARK SIDE

There is a certain duality in the human experience. There is Gabriel and Lucifer. There is pleasure and pain. There is John Wayne and the Bad Guys. There is lightness and darkness.

Everyone has a dark side or shadow self. It is our inner critic, our deepest fear, the source of our pain. People have a tendency to keep their dark side in the closet of their conscious and subconscious. It isn't something that we are proud of. We don't want to deal with it. And we most certainly don't want to reveal it.

There are many things that she stands to gain from a relationship with you, and she doesn't want to screw it up by getting into her negatives. And you are probably so blinded by the lovemaking that you can't see it or don't want to get into it either. Seeing clearly her dark side is precisely what you need to do. And the sooner you see it, the better—preferably before the sex, before she moves in, and most certainly before marriage and the babies.

Her dark side is the root of her bitchiness. It goes much deeper than a periodic down cycle. It is something that will trigger a complete turn off on you. You want to find out if she can get into and out of her dark side without trashing the relationship. You will unquestionably do time in your foxhole or take a hit while she is jousting in the darkness. The question is, will her shadow self be fatal for the two of you?

Remember that you have a dark side, too. As you need to see hers, you need to reveal yours. You may want to discuss this with her when you are both somewhat reasonable and establish a couple of rules. Rule one is that no decisions are made when someone is crazy. Rule two is that there must be at least one sane person in the relationship at all times. The relationship can survive if one of you can keep it together. Of course, the problem with this is that when you are both nuts, you are too nuts to know that you are nuts. It's not good when both people get in their dark side. Relationships usually die when this happens.

However, by embracing our shadow, we do much for ourselves. First, we better accept our whole self and our vulnerability. Second, we are able to more fully open ourselves to others. And finally, we avoid projecting our dark side on others and releasing it in violent, harmful ways. Be a friend to your shadow self.

Chapter Forty

When the Chips Are Down

You have made your bet on this woman, and have committed to a relationship with her. And now you discover that life has dealt you a difficult hand. All couples have periods of crisis. The reality of life is that life is tough.

Let's get real. You discover that she slept with Bubba. To her it's wine tasting; to you she's wine guzzling. She lets the dog eat off her plate. "No" is always "talk to your father." There is the toilet paper dilemma: does it feed from the top or bottom of the roll? Her half of the bed is the middle half. She finds all junk food tasteful, and every exercise machine distasteful. It goes on and on. Problems and difficulties are normal. To some degree, they are the usual state of affairs.

When the going gets tough, what do you do? Well, as the saying goes, the tough get going. I don't mean "bail out." I mean "get going." These situations are what define our life. They are what create opportunities for growth as human beings. They provide us, as men, the chance to demonstrate our strength and leadership in the relationship. God brings us tests; either they elevate our beliefs, or we perish.

We have some terrific tools to help us through. They may sound familiar to you. First, you can have confidence that God will somehow see you through. You know that since you are a part of God's family, things will work out. It's called **faith**. Second, you have a belief that something better will manifest in your life. You keep this dream close to you, and don't give up on it. It's called **hope**. And third, you stay focused on being loving and compassionate. When things get crazy, you can prevail, because you know who you are. You know that where you come from is good. It's called **charity**.

The true test of manliness isn't related to jumping out of airplanes with a parachute or off of a tower with a bungee cord. The solution is not to fix her. It's staying pointed in the direction of faith, hope, and charity as best you can. You can let go of fear and anxiety about what will happen, because how it turns out is up to God. You concern yourself about you; God will take care of the rest. Real masculinity is defined by the courage to overcome life's ordinary problems in an extraordinary way. Hang in there!

Chapter Forty-One

You Can't Go Back

I have listened to women say that "you can't go back." This is after they have exercised their prerogative to be liberated. They have trashed their man and their relationship. Of course, they are right at a certain level. They can't go back and relive what was done.

However, this concept doesn't go far enough. Many relationships fail because people give up too easily. They don't have the courage and support to go back. You can go back and say that you are sorry. You can go back and explain honestly what you did and why you did it, right or wrong. You can go back and tell her that you love her. If *she* screwed up, you can go back and forgive and just let it go. And if *you* screwed up, you can go back with contrition and just let it go. You can always go back.

Going back is not living in the past. It is seizing the present moment in such a way as to best move into the future. It's a good idea to do it sooner, rather than later, and to do it later, rather than never.

Maybe it will work. Maybe it will just prolong your agony in the situation. It doesn't matter. How she may or may not respond is irrelevant. What is important is that you tried. You gave it your best shot.

This is persistence. This is tenacity. This is courage. This is what being a man is all about. If she is not woman enough and enlightened enough to persist with you, so be it.

Chapter Forty-Two

Man's Best Friend

So who is your best friend? Is it your dog? Is it Jesus or Buddha? Is it your mate? Is it Bob or Monique?

Nicholas was my golden retriever; I raised him from a puppy. We hiked, ran, and backpacked together. He was there with the most unconditional love that I have ever experienced, always with a wagging tail. But after twelve years, he died. The problem with a pet as best friend is that they die.

God is good. God is great. Let us thank Him. The good thing about God is that He doesn't die. And He is a great example. But the problem with God is that life is constantly bringing us lemons. Do you know who makes the lemonade? God can show us the way, but it is up to us. God is a terrific mentor, but He is a little too perfect to be our best friend, and a little too spiritual to make really good lemonade.

I used to say that I wanted a lover, companion, and *best* friend in my mate. I think now that I was asking too much. Perhaps I should be happy with lover and companion and friend. You know it is a bummer when she has a mind change and you lose your best friend. Maybe it isn't such a hot idea to trust your mate with the best friend role.

There is the old joke about the guy telling his good buddy that he thinks that the whole world is crazy, except for the guy and his friend—and he has begun to worry about his friend. Your male and female friends all have their lives, issues, and crises. They will be there for you, unless they need to be there for themselves. It happens, and it's perfectly okay. For a review of the importance of your friends, please see chapters nineteen and thirty-five.

Who is your best friend? Guess who. It's *you*, friend. The thirty-second way to survive women's liberation is to be good to your best friend.

Chapter Forty-Three

LOOKING FOR LOVE

Are we looking for love in all the wrong places? We have debunked the notion that our best friend is our furry friend, our spiritual mentor, our drinking buddy, or our mate.

God was fairly tricky in designing the location for the kingdom of heaven. God put it in a place that is so obvious, that it is deceptively difficult to find. The kingdom of heaven is within you. The Son of God set Himself as an example, and suggested that God dwells within us. He also taught that we are to "love your neighbor, *as yourself*." The creation of our personal heaven and the ability to love begins with self love.

So how are we to be our own best friend?

One, you understand that you are a divine being, part of God's plan. You celebrate yourself as someone wonderful and unique. You remember the good that you have done. This might include a good deed, like sending your ex-girlfriend's fiancé a copy of this book.

Two, you accept that you are not perfect. By owning your own dark side, you get to move to a place of forgiveness and compassion for yourself and others. We are all just human beings, trying to do the best we can. It's not the end of the world when the guy at Slick Lube forgets to put back the plastic oil cap and it melts on your engine.

Three, you discover the good things you can do in life and make a habit of doing them. This involves finding your highest dream and/or truth, and following it. We are referring to something serious here, like hitting baseballs or saving forests or writing a man's book.

Four, you express an appreciation of yourself by being self-caring and self-pampering. No one knows how to do that better than you. It's payoff time. I kind of like something special, like a double cheeseburger at a fast food restaurant.

The better you get at loving yourself, the better you'll be at loving others, including your mate.

Chapter Forty-Four

CHIVALRY

According to the dictionary, chivalry relates to "knightly qualities." In the new age, this seems to have taken on new meaning. We have traded our shining armor for jeans and a T-shirt. Our white horse has turned into a gas-guzzling, fume-belching, horse-powered motor car with cell phone. And the closest we have come to slaying a dragon lately is poking a hamburger on the barbecue.

The Knights of the Round Table in Camelot may be fiction, but chivalry lives in the postmodern world. A woman seems to like the idea that her man is chivalrous. Men, when flattered by being told that they accomplished some chivalrous gesture, puff up. With all of the confusion about the respective roles of male and female in our society, somehow there seems to be agreement that knightly qualities are a good thing.

If chivalry lives, what is it? You should open doors and defer to a lady entering a doorway. It's also a nice idea to open her car door and push the elevator button. You should help a lady with her overcoat and travel bag. When walking with a lady, you should walk on the roadside of the walkway. This tradition dates from the times that carriages splashed and wash water was dumped on the sidewalk. A female, otherwise capable of leaping tall corporate buildings, generally wants to be helpless with these things when with her man.

I don't mind doing this stuff, but don't these gestures seem to be more a matter of social convenience? It's a good way to keep from bumping into to each other when entering a doorway or elevator.

Chivalry is not to be confused with her myth of Prince Charming. I don't know about you, but I am done with trying to be Mr. Prince Charming. One female shot my white horse, another stole my sword, and still another punched holes in my armor. "Prince Charming" is something that exists in books, movies and females' imaginations. I have asked females to define it. They are clear that they want "it," but have no clue about what "it" is. Having you live up to her fictional idea of Prince Charming is just another way for her to torment your male ego. Do you really want to chase an ill-defined, unrealistic, constantly changing, idealized notion of manhood? If so, you will be continually guessing about what the princess wants and forever defending your efforts to satisfy "it." As an alternative, perhaps you can suggest to her that you are real and you are a man. (Please notice that I did not suggest "real man." Females enjoy throwing gum in the path of any guy dumb enough to believe that he's a "REAL MAN."

So what is chivalry? The knightly qualities of courage, nobility, fairness, courtesy, and honor represent true chivalry, in a traditional sense. Perhaps these qualities are a pretty decent definition of manhood in today's world.

Chapter Forty-Five

Living Well by Living Simply

As a society we seem to be running faster and faster. We are sold on consumption and getting more and more. We have found our share of the dream all right. And we are stuck with a mortgage payment, a car payment, a credit card payment, as well as bills, bills, and more bills to show for it. We get more and more—stressed. Being a man on this treadmill is a bad deal.

A male friend of mine at the country club is getting a divorce. He made big bucks for many years in his business. The business is now in a slump, and he is in a slump with it. Guess what? His wife is exercising her prerogative to be liberated because he has turned into such a "tightwad."

This female is an example of an American princess. She defines herself by what she has, not who she is. Her self-image is based on where she has dinner, the car she drives, and the designer label on her clothes. She is special, because she has refined tastes and can spend money faster and better than the next female. Being a man with a female who sees herself as an American princess, with you as her benefactor, is an extremely bad deal.

I trust that you can clearly see the problem. So what exactly is the solution? The short answer is the title to this chapter: "Living Well By Living Simply." It is a rejection of the philosophy of winning with the most toys. It is avoiding getting involved with women who have "born to shop" at the top of their value system.

Living simply is its own reward. At its core, it recognizes that happiness comes from intangibles like giving, loving, and appreciating what you have. When you approach life with this orientation, what you have (whatever you have) is *more* than enough. The best way to get more is to appreciate what you have. You can find joy in your friendships, beauty in a sunset, enjoyment in a trip to the library, satisfaction from making love with your mate, contentment in taking a long walk, and peace from prayer. These are a few examples of pursuits that cost you nothing, and give you much. Can you live well with joy, beauty, enjoyment, contentment, and peace?

Don't get seduced by materialism, and women who never have enough. The forty-fifth way to survive women's liberation is to live well by living simply.

Chapter Forty-Six

BETTER THAN KICKING THE DOG

How do you meditate? You sit or lay down in a quiet and comfortable place. You take several slow, deep breaths and relax. You mentally move from place to place in your body and let the stress melt from your muscles. You move into a contemplative state of being.

From here, you can access your subconscious mind and accomplish wonderful things in three different ways.

First, you can use affirmations, positive statements of what you are becoming. You formulate the statement as though you had already achieved it. You state it in the meditation and let go of it, knowing that it will manifest in your life.

Second, you can remove all mental chatter to achieve a deep sense of peacefulness. One might view this form of meditation as creating a vacuum or absence of thought. This is a way to find release and to become centered.

Third, you can seek answers by asking questions and let go and trust that the reply will come. This provides a channel for dreams and visions to appear. It will give you the direction that you need to move through life.

I have just described three simple types of meditation. There are many variations on each of these basic methods. If you believe in God, meditation can be considered a process of prayer, a spiritual communication.

Meditation can be a powerful way to find direction and to move forward from a place of centeredness. Volumes have been written that expand on this subject. Masters of meditation find it perfectly complex and absolutely simple. There is no one right way for everyone. You can find your own best way to meditate. A session may take two minutes or two hours. If you work with this, it will work for you, and change your life for the better. It's simple—change your thinking, change your life.

You can vent your frustrations with her nonsense by kicking the dog. Or you can find peace and contentment through meditation. It's your choice.

P.S. As a word of caution, meditation with a negative focus will have an adverse effect. Seek the positive—truth and love.

Chapter Forty-Seven

GETTING TO COURAGE

Fear is a son of a bitch. It is what you feel when you go to war and get shot at, when you stand up in public and make a speech, when you have a panic attack, when your company is merging or downsizing, when your wife has just called her lawyer, when you can't get an erection, when you get sick, and when you're contemplating death. The bitch is your dark side. Her son is your shadow's expression through fear.

I am not referring to rational and purposeful fear. Our ancestor gets attacked by the tiger. Today, some idiot cuts you off on the highway. It triggers a fight-or-flight survival response, and that is good.

I am referring to the fear that is emotional, destructive, and debilitating: the soldier who freezes under fire, the speaker who mentally blanks to begin his talk, the person closed to some part of the world or of himself because of some phobia. We have all been there and know that it is tough.

I love the image of General Patton, in the movie, standing up to the fighter plane, saying, "Go ahead, shoot me right between the eyes, you son of a bitch." Shooting his pistol at the plane was a perfect symbol for standing down his fear. We need to embrace the fear and recognize its potential for developing character.

Whatever your fear, you are not alone in it. Somebody, somewhere, has felt it. If you need help, there is probably a support group somewhere to help you. When you are in the grip of fear, that is all you see. That is when you need to know that this is the bottom, and that in time you will move out of it. Begin with a focus on something positive. Replace your fear with healthy emotions, such as faith, hope, and charity, and move in that direction in any way possible. If you have a setback, get back to your positive focus.

Courage begins with a few baby steps in the direction of a man's highest truth. He falls down and takes a few more small steps. He stumbles, gets up, and takes a few more steps. Courage becomes the grand way of an honorable life. You are always free to take a few more steps at any time of your life. Manhood is courage.

Chapter Forty-Eight

SEXUALLY TRANSMITTED

God gave us a powerful and beautiful way to express our love and procreate. That is the good news.

Millions of people are being infected by AIDS, herpes, and other sexually transmitted diseases each year. AIDS is life-threatening and incurable. Herpes is survivable and incurable. And the other diseases, while survivable and curable, are a major source of personal and relationship anguish. All of this has reached literally epidemic proportions. That is the bad news.

You need to ask questions *before* you have sex with someone new: Do you carry the AIDS virus? Have you had sex with anyone else in the prior six months? Do you carry the herpes or HPV virus (as opposed to, are you showing any symptoms)? Have you had any other type of sexually transmitted disease and, if so, are you completely cured? If any of the answers are "yes," you need to stop, take a cold shower, and get educated about your risks. If any of the answers are "yes," you will have some element of risk.

I don't care how beautiful, wealthy, sophisticated, sexy or amorous she is. She can still have it. You need to ask (and then hope that she knows and tells the truth).

The person may not know if they have the AIDS virus, even with a test, since it may take six months to show up in the test. So-called "safe" sex is not free of risks. Although they are better than no precaution at all, condoms sometimes slip off or break. Keep in mind that if it slips while you are playing with a person carrying the AIDS virus, your life is at risk. There are more than 150,000 people with the AIDS virus in the United States, and 50,000 new cases are reported annually.

One type of incurable herpes virus can be located in an area outside the position of the condom. This means that you can be exposed to it, even with protection. A kiss can transmit another type of incurable herpes. There are more than thirty million people with the herpes virus in the United States. The HPV (genital warts) virus can be difficult to detect since the symptom is often located with the vagina or anus.

Are you prepared to explain to your mate that the cute girl at the office gave you (and possibly your mate) venereal disease? More than a quarter of a million new cases of syphilis and gonorrhea are reported in the United States each year. It happens.

Think about the risks. When in doubt, don't do it. If she exercises her prerogative, she may leave you with more than a broken heart.

P.S. If you have one of these diseases, and you want to have sex, find someone who has the same thing. Otherwise, if you don't have on these diseases and if you know what you're doing, please see chapter 101, your way.

Chapter Forty-Nine

PROTECT AND PROVIDE, AND BEYOND

Man's responsibility has been traditionally to protect and provide for his woman. The classic situation was for the man to provide money and power in exchange for the woman's beauty and sex. The deal was for the woman to be dependent and for the man to be affirmed. This was an unhappy arrangement because the woman chafed at his control, and the man resented her willingness to give (sex) in order to get. This has changed.

Women have become liberated and/or independent, and now provide for themselves. Women now make up almost half of the labor force in the United States. Society now protects our women with police officers, legal recourse, security guards, government regulation, the safety net, and national defense. It's no wonder that women see men as the icing on the cake, not the cake, and most certainly not the main course. The majority of relationships have moved beyond the protecting/providing role for the male, and there is no going back.

So what exactly have we replaced it with? One female therapist has suggested that the male purpose is now to "cherish" his woman. (Her purpose is to "respect" him.) I'm sorry, but "cherish" seems impotent compared to "provide." And that is just the problem. We have allowed ourselves to advance to the cherish role of flower bearer, fix-it guy, elevator-button pusher, and orgasm provider (at her wish). Cherish is fine, but it doesn't go far enough.

We need to take off our gym shorts, shower, and create a new, improved male role model that is more enlightened than wearing pants and more real than shinning armor. Men need to assume a leadership role in the relationship that affirms her independence and nurtures our interdependence.

This mainly has to do with moral leadership. We elevate the discussion from how to squeeze the toothpaste tube to values such as compassion. We move the standard from five star to financial independence. We affirm her self-sufficiency as a means to something more important than shopping. We let her know that we cherish commitment and exclusivity, not fickleness. Moral leadership has to do with setting the tone and culture of the relationship.

Let's elevate our place from man/servant to leader. For more on this, please see chapter eighty-nine.

Chapter Fifty

FATHERHOOD

"Mommy, if the stork delivers babies, if the tooth fairy gives money, if Santa brings toys, and if God tells us right from wrong, why *do* we need Daddy?" Indeed, why do we need Daddy? Some females of the lesbian or liberated persuasion believe that a father's involvement (beyond his sperm count) is irrelevant.

If you made them, you are responsible for them. This is true regardless of whether they arrived out of the operation of Murphy's Law or Planned Parenthood. This is also true regardless of your feelings for the woman with whom you created them—or for her divorce attorney.

At minimum, you need to do three things for your children:

First, you need to give them love. This is a privilege, because you will receive far more satisfaction from this involvement than you will give in the exchange. The love needs to be unconditional. This means that you need to let them know that you love them when they screw up, especially when they screw up. You don't need to agree with them to love them. This gives them permission to be themselves and make their own mistakes and have learning experiences.

Second, you need to be there for them. They should be a priority in your life, so that you are available if and when they need you. All of the money in the world is worthless in raising your children if you have no time for playing catch with your son or watching your daughter's dance performance. More importantly, the real test of "being there" is when they are in crisis or pain. This is true even if you are in crisis and pain. You hopefully have several friends to support you. Your children have only one Dad.

Third, you need to encourage them to follow their dreams. Your life, however you live it, will be an example to them. That example will be your primary and most important legacy. It's the most enlightened form of influence; it certainly beats rules and control, particularly as they get older. Their life gives them a God-given right to fully express their being as best they can. Your job as Dad is to encourage the expression of their gift in their way. You only fathered them; it's their life.

Being a good father is important and rewarding, even if the mother expresses her prerogative to be liberated. The rewards of fatherhood are the fiftieth way to survive women's liberation.

Chapter Fifty-One

MOTHERHOOD

One of the great joys in life is being with your mate when your baby is born. If you have been there, you know that this is a peak life experience. What usually happens after we peak?

Something happens to a women's sense of being when she gets pregnant. There is a shift that affects her priorities and outlook on life in a deep way. I call this "the Lioness

Syndrome." Very simply, the baby becomes central to her world, and you move to a place lower than before. For example, if you were fourth on her list after God, her job, and her mother, you now move into fifth place. She becomes the lioness, fiercely protective of her baby against everything, including you (the father). Figuratively, she is afraid you will eat the cubs. This aspect of motherhood is instinctive at an animal level of her being.

Most guys don't get this. They assume that once loved, always loved. She may still love you, but the depth and intensity of her caring changes when the babies come. Everyone is so busy getting the nursery ready, and then changing diapers, that this shift may not register with the guy for a while. One day, he wakes up and figures out that something has happened. He is still not sure exactly what. If he gets on a two-person raft with his wife and child in a survival mode, he will quickly come to understand. She will ask him to get in the water and swim with the sharks. ("Oh, so *that* is what is going on here!")

This is when the king of the jungle goes off to hunt solo. It's also when a guy gets serious about his job and joins his company's softball team or his community's country club. Other than having you on call for emergency runs to the store for more diapers, this is just fine with her.

I have a theory that this is a major reason why men have affairs and get mistresses. They like being number one with their woman. You might want to discuss your desire to be number one with her before you get married and start having babies. Whatever she says, human instinct is usually not suppressed for long. You deserve a fate better than a swim with Jaws.

Chapter Fifty-Two

New Itinerary for the Power Trip

It's called "the battle of the sexes." It has gone on since God created woman, and we had the great apple debacle. I can still hear Adam and Eve in the garden: "Why did you give me the apple?" "Why did you eat it?" We seem to have been set up with a power struggle from the beginning. Our challenge is to overcome it.

We have this bad habit of trying to use power to get our needs met in our relationships. The female uses her sexuality, beauty, and charm; the male uses his strength, money, and influence. When this stuff gets mixed into a play for power, they become destructive. I will provide for you, if you will give me access to your beauty. What happens when you lose your job or business? What happens when she gets a few wrinkles? This struggle for control is ultimately a losing proposition for both parties. In the end, even the "winner" will lose.

We need to move up the ladder of values in our dealings with one another. The goal of someone in a relationship shouldn't be to maximize power, control, and winning. The focus needs to be on giving, loving, and compassion.

I like the idea of coming together in a friendship, with whatever can be based on giving, loving, and compassion as a beginning. When we strip away our neediness for social status, money, or sex, we may discover the cornerstone for a solid relationship. The cornerstone can become the foundation for a much bigger, magnificent structure. This is true because the relationship is supported by values that will stand the test of time.

The relationship is based on a man and woman that is whole. Each has his/her own social status and financial independence and lovingness and lustfulness. The chemistry of two whole people coming together creates and energy that moves the couple to a higher level. This is a level beyond what the man or woman could achieve separately.

What would happen if the female contributed a measure of strength, money, and influence into the relationship? What would happen if the male's sexuality, intuition, and creativity were appreciated in the relationship? Could the relationship become empowered by both parties developing and giving more fully of their being? This would move the basis of the relationship beyond a fifty-fifty transaction, with people keeping a ledger of their contribution to a partnership so as to maintain their power and control. Man at his best has a touch of femininity. Woman at her best has a touch of masculinity. Couples at their best are consumed by the power of love, rather than the love of power.

Chapter Fifty-Three

CONNECTION

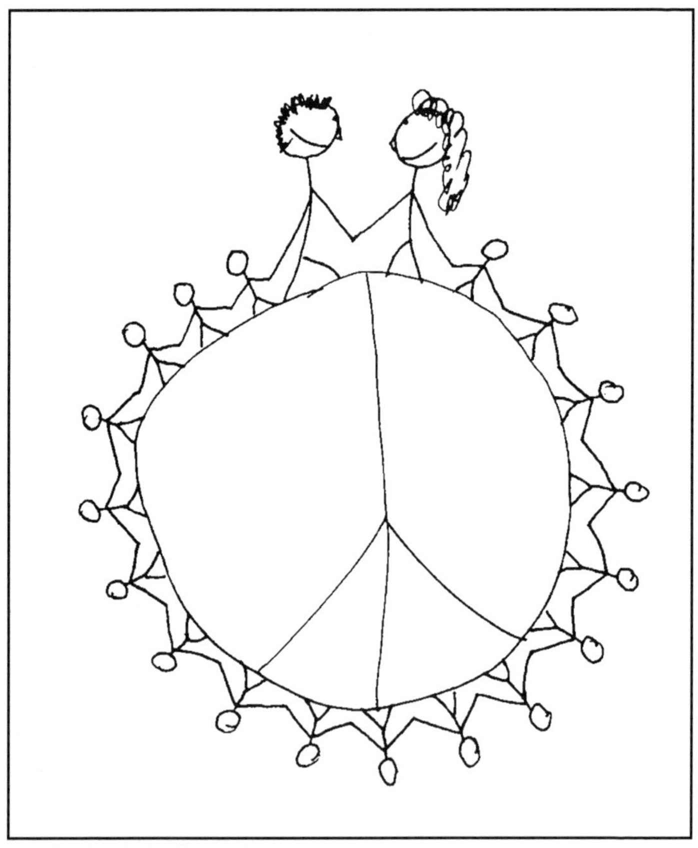

We are creating the world, and we are all in this together. An act of kindness moves the species forward and higher. A random act of hurtfulness to yourself or your mate or your neighbor is harmful to all of us. Every human interaction, kind or otherwise, inadvertent or purposeful, has meaning. Our job is to find the lesson of that interaction and to make it as positive as possible. The interaction can mirror ourselves and our issues, and provide an opportunity for self-advancement and creating good. This is important to our sense of well-being with each other and with God, since we are together on a physical and spiritual level.

We are all connected in a real, everyday sense. We can see evidence of this connection in our daily lives as the Earth shrinks with improved telecommunications and travel. We can instantly phone, FAX, or e-mail someone around the world. We have daily information from the media on significant and insignificant events in all corners of the globe. Within a day, we can travel to almost any place on Earth. We have increased togetherness as a species, for better or worse. As the closeness of this togetherness increases over time, it becomes increasingly important that it is "for better." In Los Angeles and Beirut, in Palestine, Bosnia, Somalia, South Africa, and Northern Ireland, we have witnessed the horror of "for worse." Human survival mandates harmonious connection as an evolutionary step. It will happen, because it must happen for species preservation.

This connection is true in a spiritual sense as well. The universe and all that is in it has a fundamental unity with God. As such, we are all connected within that relationship.

So what does this have to do with surviving liberation? Understanding this connection helps us see the importance of having healthy relationships. It also points out the importance of treating our mates with love and compassion. The act of her expressing liberation from a guy goes beyond the act itself. If you use and abuse her, it's more than the act itself. When we successfully survive liberation and build loving relationships, there are implications for all of us as we move together up the evolutionary pathway. All men are our brothers. And all women are our sisters and lovers. We can move our collective connection a little closer to the Almighty.

Chapter Fifty-Four

HER NAGGING

Penis envy is why some females nag us. It has nothing to do with what they are nagging us about. It is just the female way of acting out their jealousy. Some females nag because of emotional damage and insecurity. You might file this propensity to nag in the "other female nonsense" category.

Most females maintain something called "the List." The things she is nagging you about can be without basis in reality. An example might be something like, "Our water is unfit for consumption." Of course, the neighbors, the dog, and the plants haven't died, and they all drink the stuff. The List can have a touch of reality and logic, and still be without merit. An example of this could be, "The dog has fleas." The dog may have fleas, but you just washed the damn dog with a mix of bug killer and toilet bowl cleaner the day before. "Give it a rest, sweetheart; I handled it," you say. The point is that her List does not need to make sense.

You may find it helpful to keep in mind what the List is really about—her envy and/or hurt. This will help you keep some perspective about what's on it. If you try to do everything that comes up on it, you will end up in the mental hospital. I trust that you understand the implications of what I'm saying here. Don't get crazy about the items that she puts on it. If you do everything, you will give power to the List. Ninety days from now, there will be a new List. Another characteristic of her List is that it is never ending.

So what do you do about the nagging? Just understand that the poor thing can't help herself, and be compassionate. If it gets miserable, please remember to "keep your head down" (see chapter twenty-five).

What hurts is when she exercises her prerogative and takes her List on the road in search of the greater fool/man/servant.

Please understand that it is enough that you understand the basis of her nagging. If you confront her reasons for nagging, you will lose big time. This isn't to say that the envy and hurt don't exist. It's just that she will disqualify you from today's game as an insensitive chauvinist, and you will score no more points.

P.S. Why do men die before their wives? They want to!

Chapter Fifty-Five

LIVING SOULFULLY

I learned as a child that a "soul" was like a score sheet. The good deeds showed up as white spots; the sins were like black marks that could be erased by confession, if we were really sorry. If we had a mostly white soul when we died, we would go to heaven. The black souls were sent by God to hell, so you had better be a good boy.

I don't believe in this black and white stuff any more. A compassionate God would not send a being to burn for eternity. I believe in a compassionate God.

A "soul" is a human creation to symbolize our connection with something that we know and do not fully understand—God. When we live soulfully, we are living in a way that is connected with God. This way of living is something that we grasp intuitively, a deep and powerful inner knowing. This connection is a good and comforting way to live, especially since we are human and are always screwing up.

I believe God understands that we are all here doing the best we can, given what God gave us to work with. God, who is by definition "perfect," understands this. Can't we all lighten up and be a little more accepting and loving of each other? I can imagine God sitting in heaven with a Christian Brothers' brandy and his feet up on a cloud, going on about what mayhem those idiots (us) are doing to each other now. I believe God wants us to make it a little easier for ourselves. God gave us a fairly simple message: "Love each other."

We are all part of the Divine Being, sons and daughters of God. We create our own heaven and hell on this Earth in our life. If we lie, cheat, steal, hate, damage, envy, kill, slander, and generally abuse our fellow man and Mother Earth, it will come back to us. If we can connect with God in a place of love and compassion, it will have its own reward in our lives.

So how does women's liberation fit with "love each other?" Let's review the libber's motto: "I loved you yesterday, but I became unfilled, and so now I am liberated and full of pride, and don't forget my alimony check, you cheap bastard." I'm sorry, but I just don't think that it fits well at all. The challenge is to try living soulfully with liberation. After all, She (what if the sum of Father, plus Son, plus Holy Ghost equals "She," not "He?" That should keep some ivory tower guy busy for awhile) wants us to love libbers too!

Chapter Fifty-Six

Bliss

Bliss is work, loved. It is not really work unless you would prefer doing something else. I believe that we should do what we love to do, in career and in life. If you are doing something you enjoy, you will eventually become good at it. People who are enthusiastic about expressing their special ability are a joy to behold. Although money often rewards talent, it is secondary to someone who is pursuing his bliss. What is important is that we have spent our precious lifetime "working" on something that we enjoyed. Find your passion in life and follow it.

Men often define themselves by how much money they make. They get on a treadmill of wants. Their women are with them so long as the treadmill keeps going around. And when the treadmill slows down or stops, the woman becomes liberated. Or we stay on the treadmill and it keeps going faster and faster, to a point of burnout and emotional crisis. We look at ourselves and start asking what we are doing with our lives. Why am I not happy? We bottom out and eventually come back to the idea of nurturing self and finding our true passion in life.

It is important to disconnect money as the controlling force in our lives. We do that by selecting a woman who is self sufficient, and not by buying her. We do that by following our passion, not by working to maximize our paycheck. We do that by living simply, with an investment plan that will give us financial independence. When we take these steps, we start moving down life's path with some real choices. We can begin to see life as a channel for God expressing through us. We find ways to give in a manner that will be uplifting and rewarding. Bliss is one element in the balance between our relationships, community involvement, spirituality, and self-nurturing.

Another way to survive liberation is to find bliss and balance in our lives.

Chapter Fifty-Seven

COMMUNITY

Involvement with our community brings us out of selfishness and integrates us into our greater neighborhood. This provides the opportunity to share ourselves and to give something back to our fellow man. Nothing is completely altruistic. The act of giving to the community comes back to us with a feeling of self-satisfaction that we are able to do something good. This involvement also gives us the chance to share skills and talent that we might otherwise not be able to express. If we are fortunate, we will actually accomplish something meaningful for society.

Involvement with our community usually means that we are participating with a group of people having a common mission or goal. This purpose is a good greater than ourselves. And the organization of a group effort allows us to be a part of something that is beyond what we can accomplish individually. Examples are: caring for the ill, expressing the arts, athletic competition, educating our youth, community service, spiritual enrichment, feeding the hungry, and political activism. This gives us the opportunity to explore our unique interests with the friendship and support of a group.

We usually get out of this involvement as much or more than what we put into it. Ask not what your community can give you, ask what you can give your community.

Community involvement, like loving self, living soulfully, nurturing a diversity of personal relationships, and following our bliss, is another way to add richness to our life. By achieving a balance in these areas of life, we can put liberation in proper perspective, namely see it as a triviality—and thereby survive it.

Chapter Fifty-Eight

Custody Rights

Why do the courts assume that men are second-class parents? The courts generally accept the feminist belief that the father's day-to-day involvement is simply not important to the child's development. When it comes down to it, the female usually gets primary custody of the kids and the male gets the child support payments and visitation. This can work, but is it fair? As one dad said, "I'm not a paycheck; I'm a father."

I understand that men are not very good at breast-feeding. Beyond that, however, most men make damn good parents. Dads can and do love their children. With males and females now equally participating in the work force, the dad often has as much time to care for the children as the mom does. Society has changed, but the old child custody traditions have not kept up with those changes. They are based on a model of the workplace and typical family that no longer exists.

Today's child custody and support negotiations are structured to be unfair to the man. This is because his default position has two unpleasant outcomes: losing custody of the children and making child support payments. The woman's default position (or path of least resistance) has two pleasant outcomes: keeping the children and receiving child support payments. This should be changed to an equal or level default position. That is, if a parent wants the benefit of custody of the children, that parent should pay for the support. This approach levels the playing field for custody and support negotiations.

In my view, the divorcing parents should set the child support payments, not the court. First, the parents are given the option to accept shared custody and no support. If this alternative is not workable, each parent is offered primary custody without support from the other parent. If neither of these options is acceptable, the negotiation would work like a bid. For example, the man offers the woman one hundred dollars per month if she takes primary custody. She says "no" and offers him one hundred dollars per month if he takes primary custody. He says "no" and offers her two hundred dollars per month if she takes primary custody. This process continues, with the amount increasing until one parent agrees to the terms. The winning parent takes custody of the children the old-fashioned way—he or she earns it.

Mom and Dad could conceivably sit down and work this out in fifteen minutes. Of course, the lawyers wouldn't be appreciative, because it's simple and people can figure it out on their own. It cuts the lawyers out of the negotiations, and their tendency to keep everyone angry with outrageous back-and-forth settlement offers that go on and on. People will have more of a tendency to honor their "commitments" if they participate in making them. Admittedly, this is the way it should be. This is not the way it is.

Again, the reality is that she typically gets the kids, and you get to make the support payments. If you are considering having children, you will want to think about the possibility of her going lib with the kids. If that happens, you will want to have some idea of your financial responsibilities and where you want to go with the custody. Please review chapter thirty-three on pregnancy and Murphy's Law in this context. Understanding your exposure to the downside of liberation and your rights or lack of rights in dealing with it is an important survival technique.

Chapter Fifty-Nine

DRUGS AND BOOZE

If you have a problem with drugs and booze, get the problem under control before you get into a relationship. Otherwise, she will likely exercise her prerogative sooner or later and then you will have two problems: getting over the breakup, and the addiction. The trauma of the loss may make it more difficult for you to deal with the addiction. If you have an addiction problem, she will be justified in leaving—maybe.

The "maybe" has to do with who and what she is. She probably would not have gotten involved with you knowing you had the problem, unless she herself had a problem (not necessarily your problem). In this case, you deserve each other and the living hell that you create for each other. You will be in a better place for selecting a mate if you take care of your problem before you get involved.

You may decide to persist with your addiction in a relationship. That is your choice. What is unfortunate is the impact that it will have on your children. They deserve better.

Our lives are nothing more than an expression of what happens in our conscious and subconscious mind. When we foul our minds with drugs and booze, we foul our lives. You can't pick up a newspaper without reading about somebody who got high and got killed. Drug overdoses and drunk-driving accidents happen. More than the headlines, the real tragedy is the lives that were lived with the pain of unfulfilled dreams.

My only suggestion is to face your problem and to understand that many other people have faced the same problem. You are not alone with this, and you can get better. Get into a support group and stay with it. You deserve better.

Chapter Sixty

LIFE IS RIGHT

Life isn't wrong. If you are struggling with life, life is right. It's you who are wrong. Life is a perfect flow. Yes, I know that there are ripples, waves, and storms along the way. If you are struggling with it, you are probably paddling against the current. It's much better to find a way to have the current work with and for you.

If a woman wants to be liberated, let her go. If a woman wants to be independent, embrace her self-sufficiency and find ways to benefit from it. These are two examples of working with the flow.

There is an old cliché that says, "If you can't beat them, join them." No one wins a relationship power struggle. Eventually, the combatants beat each other up, and the winner goes away losing, because the loser is hurt and bitter. Try to step away from the struggle and redefine it in a way that everyone can win. Use the person's energy to your advantage, rather than fighting it. Find a way to win with them.

At any given time, there are positive and negative flows, something is going up and something is going down. Our job is to get out of the way of the negative and move with the positive. This does not mean following the path of least resistance, or taking the easy way out. "Positive" means seeking the truth, the moral high ground in a situation, and putting our energy in that direction. What is right may seem like it is against the flow at the time. It may not be the most popular or expedient choice. But given time, you always want to be on the side of the highest truth, the ultimate positive flow. Using the alternative to dog kicking (meditation) and plugging into your masculine intuition (sixth sense) are helpful in feeling the right course.

It isn't what happens to us; right and wrong things will happen. That's life. What is important is how we interpret those events. As men, we want to find the lesson in the situation and turn it into something positive for us and for the people around us. Life is right. Our function is to find what is right in it for us. If life brings you lemons, make lemonade.

This may help you move beyond liberation as frustration, into a place of contentment.

Chapter Sixty-One

FUNNYMAN

Sometimes you just have to laugh. Life gets so crazy that you need to find the humor in it just to survive. So what is so humorous about some poor guy having a hemorrhoid operation?

Funnyman is a part of manhood that goes way back and runs real deep. Can you envision the cavemen sitting around the fire laughing about the trick that they used to capture the woolly mammoth, or about the latest sick joke from the guy in the next cave? The good feeling that comes from a good laugh is at the core of the human experience.

We men have gotten accomplished at this in many ways. There is the humorist, jester, clown, joker, trickster, comic, and magician. Whatever the means, we poke fun at the elevated and uplift the downtrodden.

Men do not need training in being funny. This comes naturally to most guys, if females would only recognize it. Examples are:

- drinking milk from the carton
- thinking about having sex with her 90% of the time.
- fixing the car, lawn mower, or other home equipment
- watching six T.V. shows, including three games at once.
- finishing the ice cream without a major proclamation
- healing sports injuries without emergency medical care
- putting on the underwear with the hole or holes
- looking cool getting from the bedroom to the bathroom while aroused
- saving on the food budget by going hunting or fishing
- transforming the barbecued chicken into toast
- beating her boss at his game
- adjusting its position poorly disguised as hunting for keys
- bringing home five items, none of which were on her list
- complimenting her mother on her liposuction
- running into "hidden" objects while looking at body parts
- taking off her brassiere, gracefully
- creating colorful tie-dye effects by mixing laundry.

Women need to give us a little slack when we do such manly and funny things.

The beauty of being a trickster is that we can master the impossible. We can be he-man and funnyman at the same time.

As a survival technique, laughter is right up there with eating ice cream and enjoying auto-eroticism.

P.S. Why does it take one million sperm to fertilize one egg? They won't stop to ask for directions.

Chapter Sixty-Two

Sixth Sense

Women are not the only ones with intuitive powers. Men are intuitive also. As men, we need to understand that this is our birthright and a part of our being. This is an important sense that we access through our heart, gut, and soul. It may speak to us in a dream, in meditation, or in the shower. It may feel right. It may feel wrong. But we know it to be true at a deep, spiritual level.

You can read about it in a book. But it is not something that you know through any of your five senses. It is not something that you know from social norms or from the ten commandments. A mentor may point you in the general direction, but it isn't something that can be taught. This is a feeling that is unique and personal to you.

This sixth sense is a channel to your soul and your relationship with your higher power. It is important to be open to what it is telling you. That is why creating space in your life for prayer and meditation is so important. It gives you the opportunity to be in touch with your feelings and hopefully with what God is telling you. If we are being willful and grinding out our single-minded focus, there will be no place for soulfulness to move into and through our lives.

This sixth sense is the way to your truth. Your truth may differ from my truth. Your truth is what intuitively feels right or wrong for you. This may evolve and develop as you go through life and learn the lessons that it brings. Hopefully, this evolution brings an increasing wisdom and a clearer sense of our highest truth. There is no book, especially this book, that is the whole truth. Each of us has a special pathway to a discovery of his relationship with God and to an understanding of his truth.

Her rules, the List, and other forms of female nonsense have no power over your pathway unless you give them that power. What happens when you let go of your ego and allow the power of the ultimate Good to express itself through you? You tell me.

Chapter Sixty-Three

THE BIG BANG

We can draw an interesting lesson from the study of astronomy and history. The lesson is that somehow the Earth keeps spinning and life goes on.

Advances in astrophysics are unraveling the mysteries of the universe. We can now see the universe as the rapid expansion of a large scattering of diverse objects. This expansion will continue until the gravitational pull sucks all of this back into a major black hole. This will eventually create a singularity of matter and energy that sets the stage for the ultimate big one—the Big Bang. The time, space, and enormity of all this excites and stretches the imagination.

The history of the universe sets the context for the history of man. It is interesting to reflect on the evolution of our species from lower forms of life to our current "advanced" intellect. We have been the ape man, the caveman, the ice man, the renaissance man, and more recently the company man and the computer nerd. Some guy actually lived, struggled, loved, laughed, and died—six thousand years ago, four thousand years ago, and two thousand years ago—so you and I can get up tomorrow and go to Disneyland. This is amazing—really incredible.

What is the importance of the toothpaste squeeze issue in this context? You are annoyed that she has a headache, again. You are furious about the call from her divorce attorney, again. I'm sorry, but our sniveling emotion is fairly insignificant in the ultimate scheme of things. When we see the big picture, perhaps we can put our worries and concerns in context. Maybe they aren't such a big deal after all. Life goes on, and we need to go on with it.

Relative to the big bang and our place in history, the travails of her foolishness are meaningless.

Chapter Sixty-Four

I Love You

The liberated woman boldly asks God why He made her so soft. And God replies, "So that man will love you." Next she asks God why He made her with such lovely curves. And God replies, "So that man will love you." She compliments God on what a terrific job He did in creating her. Feeling good about

His fine work in making woman, she asks God why He made man so stupid. And God replies, "So that man will love you."

Love is an expression of heart and preferably, but not necessarily, also an expression of mind. Tell her that you love her. Tell her again. Try to tell her at least once a day. You need to let her know that you care and that she is special to you. These are the three most important words in any language.

When it comes to loving a woman, I like to engage the "K.I.S.S. Rule." You know: Keep It Simple, Stupid. Give yourself to her physically and emotionally in a way that is intense, passionate, and unconditional. Love her. All a good woman wants is for you to love her—*really* love her.

Some females believe that "diamonds are a woman's best friend." If she gets your ability to provide money, babies, social standing, security, entertainment, toys, and so forth confused with your ability to love her, that is her problem. Hopefully, you will discover her problem before you get trapped by the "M" word. As Mae West once said, "A man in love is like a clipped coupon—it's time to cash in."

To love a woman is to take her in our arms and feel that she breathes with us, errors with us, suffers with us, and loves with us. The most common acts are made beautiful through love.

"I love you." It's the sixty-fourth way to survive you-know-what.

Chapter Sixty-Five

Gift Items

I am opposed to buying a women's affections.

"I love you." It's cheaper than flowers, better for her figure than chocolates, more personal than stones, and more environmentally aware than a fur coat. She will argue to the death that these are good gift items, so don't try to explain to her your reasoning.

Sexy night clothes are definitely a bad gift item. If you get caught with the lingerie catalogue, you are suspected and guilty of one strike. If you suggest something from it, the item will never be right for her. Also, it leaves you vulnerable to her sucking you into a comparison of the blonde's great body in the catalogue and the brunette with the great body on the next page. This is a sure strike two. If you are stupid enough to actually buy her something sexy, you will get the "all you're interested in is sex" thing. It's strike three and you're out.

If you didn't know already, a blender, a vacuum cleaner, or most anything mechanical for the garage is not a good substitute for "I love you." In fact, these gifts will probably earn you a burned dinner and serious negative points.

So what do you get her? I would suggest that you make her a special card. When I say "make," I mean you sit down with some card stock and colored pens and actually create something. Even an artistic idiot can draw hearts and flowers. Or you might attempt to develop your green side and plant a rose and/or flower garden. Women love to get flowers—especially something that you have had a hand in growing. Another way is to ask her for a list of the items that she would really like and use it as a starting point. What's most important is that you remember to get *something*, especially on her birthday, your anniversary, Valentine's Day, and Christmas. These special occasions are mandatory gift days. However, the best gift item is a surprise that is associated with nothing other than your love. This will earn you major positive points.

The princess rolls over in bed, wakes up her man, and says, "Oh sweetheart, I just dreamed that you bought me a lovely diamond necklace."

Immediately seeing the trap, the guy responds, "Go back to sleep, darling, and enjoy it."

Chapter Sixty-Six

If It Feels Good . . .

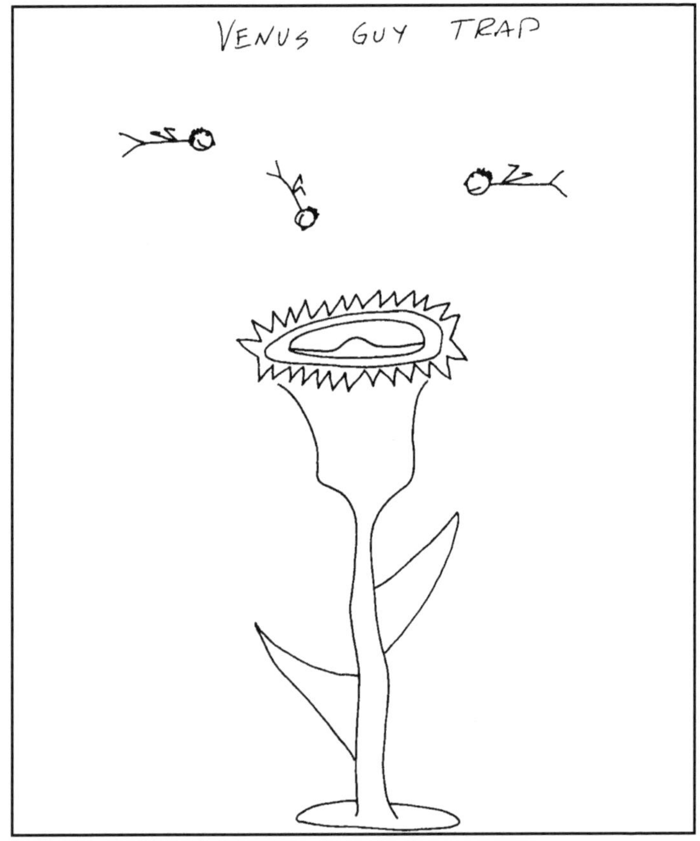

Out of fairness, I should disclose my predisposition toward sex. My mother and father christened me with the baptismal name "Randy." The old English meaning of "randy" (with a small "r") is "horny." Most men suffer from this condition; I just happen to have been named for it. Frequency of sex can be a major problem for a man. I have a secret solution for this that, in and of itself, should sell lots of books. Read on.

God made man with the express purpose to pollinate the flower. This is basic. Without this, we don't survive as a species. We men are like bees, perpetual-movement beings, always buzzing around with an insatiable need for nectar. The difficulty is that the flower is constantly moving (in her BMW convertible), unpredictably opening and closing, and sometimes (usually when you least expect it) morphing into a Venus Guy Trap. As you may know, the Venus trick is serious because it can be life threatening to the male when we are consumed.

Do you remember when you met her? She was the undiscovered starlet working in the local deli. Or the starving artist. Or the struggling designer. Those were the days; making love twice a weekday and thrice on Sunday. You were such a sweet, darling, lovable man in her eyes. You asked her to move in or even get married, and, joy, she did! This brings us to the natural state of male/female affairs. You soon find out that you are overpowering her sexuality. The issue is never that she is underpowering your sex drive. She labels you a single-minded sex addict who obviously needs therapy. The sad aspect of this is that you love her and wish to express it. And to make matters worse, she smells good, looks good, and feels good, and she sleeps next to you.

You are again in a no-win situation, and this is what I suggest you do. Find a copy of any "how to" sex book. It will be something with a title like *Living on Love: A Gourmet Guide to Sex for Breakfast, Lunch, and Dinner*. Read it, give it to her, and say that you want to talk. Do you recall all those damn books on "communication in relationship" that she keeps giving you? I'm not suggesting that this book will actually do any good on the frequency-of-sex problem, but at least you can get some revenge on the communication issue. If you actually sit down to talk about the book, please be careful, because the discussion may quickly move from six times a week, to your addiction, to her favorite "honey do" project.

If the book and conversation fail, try this fall-back position: take a cold shower and go fishing with your best buddy to your favorite lake. Maybe you'll get lucky.

Chapter Sixty-Seven

Sex—An Understanding

What happens in bed is often an expression of what is going on between you and your mate more generally. This expression can be beautiful, hurtful, exciting, mindless, giving, selfish, gentle, boring, or pleasurable. It gets complicated when we bring all of this stuff into the lair. This complexity creates a richness, but it can also cause misunderstandings, hurt feelings, and exasperation.

Don't let the complexity confuse you, or you will be subject to her rule. You recall that her rule is that she is ready when she is ready, and you are to be ready all the time. You can do better than this. Isn't there a vision that will raise her perspective to create a better place for both of you? You need to be clear as to where you stand on this.

The idea of a relationship is that you are in it to love and nurture each other. You are there for each other, to give and receive. Lovemaking is a part of this exchange. If she wants to have sex, you are there for her. If you want to have sex, she is there for you. The orientation is to be there for your partner. This moves beyond excuses, headaches, fickleness, and an arbitrary number of times per week. This avoids the "you were a jerk yesterday" issue. I mean, so what? Yesterday was yesterday, and today is today. This prevents the use of sex as a weapon or favor to get other needs met. This elevates labels like "sex on demand" to "full acceptance of your loving expression." This affirms sex for what it is: a MUTUALLY pleasing exchange. Fundamentally, the orientation is to be there for your partner.

What is fair is fair. You are there for her. She is there for you. If this makes sense to you, make sure that she understands that this is what you expect. Ask her for a commitment to this orientation. She will give it to you, because you are committing to be there for her. If she rejects the commitment, you have learned something very valuable, hopefully sooner rather than later.

By signing a copy of this chapter, you signify that you agree with the above guidelines concerning sexual activity.

AGREED:

____________________ ____________________

Woman Man

Chapter Sixty-Eight

LIFE AS QUEST

Life is a quest. We are on a journey to find ourselves, so that we can fully express our special gift.

An example of this comes from the Bible, when Jesus spent forty days and nights in the desert. He had his meeting with the devil and defined his place in the world and in history. This is symbolic of the human experience. We all meet with the devil sooner or later, in one way or another on our pathway. The result of the meeting will determine who we are and what we are about. We come back from our stay in the desert either as our own man, or captivated by the demonic forces. This may sound dramatic, but it is being played out everyday in our lives.

Another way to look at this is through our passage from childhood to manhood. You will recall your experience as a teenager. We have this intense need for independence and rebellion, and a tendency to learn by screwing up. It is a right of passage that we all experience. We need to establish ourselves as a differentiated individual before we can return home and be fully integrated into the community. Some of us never leave; some never reconcile their meeting with the devil and become individuals, and some never return home from the journey. These people usually live tragic lives.

Many of us have this quest backwards when it comes to a relationship with a women. We start out trying to find a female before we have found ourselves. You know the married guy at the office, the one who caught the cute skirt last week? You know the other married guy at the office who is pecked, as in "henpecked"? You know the single guy who has a code to personally screw down everything that moves. Could it be that each of these guys doesn't know himself or have a clue about what he wants? The classic quest in mythology usually involves departing on a pilgrimage, experiencing some initiation process, and returning home completed. This is *your* quest. You will want to be wary of anyone or anything who has the answers ready for you. We need to define ourselves as men before we go off on the hunt for a woman. By doing this, you will make a better choice and save yourself a lot of grief.

A liberated man or woman is a person on the quest who hasn't come back.

Chapter Sixty-Nine

LOVE AS DECISION

Isn't romantic love wonderful? It's hearts and flowers, moonlight and candlelight, and making love till the wee hours. But you know what? As captivating as that is, it's not what love is really about.

Love is a decision.

People get overpowered with the romance and with the feeling of being in love. And when the feelings stop, the love stops. I'm sorry, but that is just plain immature. The implications of that immaturity for our society are divorce, broken families, and emotional pain. It's sad.

I am not going to suggest that women are the only ones who change their minds in a committed relationship. But it is a women's prerogative, and I see females do it time and time again. I have observed in real life the following reasons for a female to change her mind about you: your getting a pot belly, your drinking too much, your making too little money, your growing apart from her, your losing a job, your refusing to redecorate your already-redecorated house, your working too hard, your not working hard enough, your being cheap, your not supporting her decision to quit her job. Oh, I almost forgot, your love handles. Each of these are "no fault" reasons for her to trash your relationship. Her "commitment" is a commitment for only so long as she feels warm and fuzzy about you.

I call this "the Female Fickleness Factor." A survey was done on men's and women's attitudes toward staying with or not staying with their mate. For a wide variety of reasons, women were willing to leave 15 to 20 percent more frequently than men.

"No fault" does not mean irresponsible and unreasonable. Did she make a commitment to the relationship? Whatever happened to "for richer or for poorer, in sickness and in health, until death do us part?"

Again, the point is that love is a decision. Please review chapter twelve, "Commitment and Compassion." It's called loyalty. Does she really understand that love is, at its most basic level, making a decision and sticking with it?

Chapter Seventy

PURPOSE

Having purpose in life beats the alternative. Having life without purpose may lead to the alternative. If you don't know where you're going, you probably won't get there. Your purpose needs to be general enough so that the best alternatives get incorporated and specific enough so that it's meaningful.

Here are some ideas that might make a good purpose:

- Express life with peace and contentment.
- Find a need and fill it.
- Live simply and well
- Love life and let life love me.
- Think globally, act locally.
- Use my God-given talents to achieve my highest expression.
- Love myself and my neighbor.
- Harmonize with the energy of the universe.

A purpose is like a new suit of clothes. You may want to try it on for a while and see how it feels. It needs to be tailored to get a good fit.

The wonderful and scary thing about purpose is that when you state it with clarity, it usually becomes manifest in your life within a short time. The important part of this is "clarity." You need to be clear about what you want. You want to be careful about this. It should be something positive for you and for the people in your life. The good and bad news may be that you get what you wanted. "DBA" doesn't stand for "doing business as" in this context. It stands for desire, belief, and acceptance. For your purpose to work in your life, you need three things:

Desire—you must want it.

Belief—you must believe that you can get it.

Acceptance—you must be willing to accept getting it.

When you have these three things working together, you will have a clarity of purpose. When this happens, stand back, because something extraordinary is going to happen.

This is your life's purpose. Try to find something from the heart. Pick something significant. So who are you? And what are you doing here?

Chapter Seventy-One

GOALS

Happiness is that place in life where you catch up with the carrot. Or is it?

Another approach to finding purpose in life is "bottoms up." You let your highest expression come by default from the mix and summation of achieving your goals. This assumes that you have some goals. What is "DBA" for self, community, bliss, relationships, and spirituality?

You sit down with a blank sheet of paper and jot down what you want in each of these areas. If you wish to get sophisticated, you could do it for the short-term (one year) and long-term (five years). However, the important thing is that you do it and update it around New Year's Day.

Examples are:

Self
- Find a need. Learn about computers. Take a class.
- Love self. Get fit. Work out four times a week.
- Think globally. Go to Africa. Read a travel book.
- Simplify life. Get rid of the garage junk.

Community
- Give back. Participate in this year's school fund-raiser.

Bliss
- Find a need and fill it. Give the client more than expected.
- Love life. Devote fifteen minutes a day to your passion.

Relationships
- Use God-given talents. Coach your daughter's sports team.
- Life loves you. Live simply. Take your son on a hike.
- Achieve highest expression. Date your mate once a week.
- Love a neighbor. Call or write a friend once a week.

Spirituality
- Harmonize with the Energy. Meditate three minutes a day.
- Love self. Commit to a daily affirmation.

Having goals provides direction, not necessarily happiness. When I get the new car, the next promotion, the mortgage paid off, the flat stomach, the tall blond—then I'll be happy. This doesn't work, because we never quite get there. We are always chasing the next carrot, booked solid with activity. Happiness is that place in life where you find peace and contentment with the process of being, just being

You now have your goals, and, taken together, your purpose. This is the process of converting your dreams into reality. Again, happiness has more to do with enjoying the journey than with the destination. It's your life. Perhaps you have a higher calling than serving the princess or worshipping the goddess. Be your own man.

Chapter Seventy-Two

THE ZONE

We're talking philosophy here. The reason that we need philosophers is to elevate and clear our thinking.

Plato taught that we can achieve knowledge by our reason, the human ability to think. Our reason tells us that there is love, beauty, joy, truth, as well as hate, sin, sadness, and evil in the world. This might be considered a more cerebral, spiritual, and idealistic approach to life; nonsexual, nonphysical relationships are called "platonic."

Aristotle, Plato's student, taught that we can achieve knowledge by or through our senses, through an empirical and systematic study of our surroundings. We know it, because we sense (touch, smell, see, hear, and taste) it. This can be viewed as a more practical or sensual way of knowing life. Suggesting that "the best way to a man's heart is through his stomach" might be an example of this.

Have you had a day when everything goes right? You were in the zone. I know this from athletics. I once pitched a no-hit baseball game in little league. It is the feeling of mind, body, and spirit "being in the flow." It could be a period of time, an event, or a project during which you were "grooved." Ideally, we want the zone to be a place of permanence.

So what does the "zone" have to do with Plato and Aristotle? I believe that we get to the zone by using a two-step process. First, we select an activity that requires a challenge. We use positive visualization to create routines that cue the activity and turn the power of emotions into the positive energy necessary to drive the activity. This is the platonic method. Second, we just let go and feel it happen. Reasoned thinking, negative chatter, mental distractions, expectations are all minimized. This is an Aristotelian approach. This two-step process enables you to create and expand your time in the zone.

The zone is a place for you to transcend her nonsense. When you are in the flow, why fret about liberation?

P.S. If a man speaks in the woods and his mate is not there to hear him, is he still wrong?

Chapter Seventy-Three

You Can't Live With Them . . .

. . . and you can't live without them. At one time I actually believed this. Now, I believe that this is part of a sinister plot started by pinko liberal feminists to confuse and befuddle men. Feminists will probably claim that they don't need a plot to do this, because men are already confused and befuddled.

You know what? They are probably right on that, judging by how many men actually try to follow their rules.

The part that says "you can't live with them" may be true. Since females always retain their prerogative, there is always the possibility that you can't live with them. Keeping this understanding central to your dealings with women is helpful. If used, it can minimize our vulnerability to the damage and loss that results from their mind change.

The part that says "you can't live without them" is absolutely false. It creates a damned if you do, damned if you don't dilemma that is designed to make men crazy. The truth is that you most certainly *can* live without them. If you listen to liberated women, they sure as hell can live without you.

She loves me; she loves me not. It's now "loves me not." You have fallen from your Prince Charming pedestal. You recall that her decision is no-fault. And besides, she is fully "justified," since you lost your money, lost your hair, and found your belly. What is important to remember is that you can live without her. Love isn't lost or found; it's created.

This can be fun! This is an opportunity to throw open the window shade, smell the fresh air, and start a new day with renewed enthusiasm. This is a time in your life when your loss is actually a win in hiding. This is a perfect time to reconnect with your soul and, in the process, rediscover your love. You get to again do life when you want, if you want, and how you want. This is a good thing. Enjoy!

Chapter Seventy-Four

P.M.A.

What do you do when your dog dies? What happens when your mate exercises her prerogative? Your child just brought home three D's and two F's. It's a dead-battery day. You've had a nasty bug for three months, and feel like hell. She has DMS or PMS and you are stuck in your foxhole. Bad stuff happens. So now what?

Life is 99 percent attitude and 1 percent reality. Life is not so much the reality; it is how we deal with the reality. The reality is tough. And the ability to keep a positive mental attitude in the face of reality is tougher. But that is the challenge of being a man and of being a happy man.

It is all in your mind. You have the power to envision what you want to come into your life. You have the power to transform whatever is in your life into something good. We do that by meditation (prayer) to get in touch with our soul and to discover our true, divine self. Using creative visualization, we define a dream or desire of where we want to be. Using affirmations, we bring this dream or desire into reality. When bad stuff happens, we use these techniques to stay focused on the positive areas of our life.

It is so easy to get on the treadmill and move at a speed that causes a loss of our inner self. It's like we are experiencing 99 percent reality and 1 percent attitude—negative. This is self defeating, since we are getting back the negativity that we are putting out. We need to slow down when this happens. We need to create the time to nurture our mental attitude, with a focus on affirmative values, such as loyalty, love, and laughter.

Mankind is interconnected in a common consciousness. As the Earth shrinks and the human race moves to this interconnected place in a more loving and positive way, I believe that truly wonderful things will happen. Our species will evolve to a friendlier, happier, and higher spiritual place.

A Positive Mental Attitude (P.M.A.) can keep you from letting her nonsense move you into a negative state. This is man as a good and positive being.

Chapter Seventy-Five

FIGHTING FAIR

The main thing that you need to understand about fighting with a female is that it is not about furthering communication and agreement. It may originate from her need to relieve herself of frustrations having nothing or something to do with you. It may be about her down cycle of the moment. It is typically about something totally dumb and insignificant (which becomes apparent the following day). She just feels like fighting. It is important to understand that you have a choice with this. You can elect to get out of the way and get in your foxhole (see chapter twenty). Or if you happen to be in the mood, you can duke it out with her.

A good fight can be healthy for a relationship. I am referring to a yelling and screaming, get it all out, ranting and raving argument. Both parties get to vent negative energy, and this is what a good fight is all about. All relationships create a tension that builds over time. Good communication doesn't always cut through the tension. That is when a good fight can be beneficial. It can provide a magical breakthrough and release.

I am not referring to something that gets physically abusive or involves property damage. I am not referring to one of those arguments that plays back time after time with no resolution. I am not referring to one of those discussions that ends with hurt feelings and people leaving mad. The danger of giving expression to your negative energy is that it becomes habitual. The drama and excitement of fighting can become addictive.

Although a good fight isn't about communication and agreement, a successful fight does need a measure of resolution. You get it off your chest. You get to say exactly what's been bothering you. You get to express fully. And now we are done. And now we feel better.

I was in a relationship with a lady for many years. Our fights are one of my fondest memories of her. She could fight well and fair. Verbally, we would both push and pull. "Damn it, your [whatever] makes *me* crazy." "Yeah, well your [whatever] makes me crazy." We didn't necessarily solve problems or resolve issues. But when we were done, we were done, and there was the best lovemaking imaginable. I haven't seen her for years, and I still love her for that.

The seventy-fifth way to survive women's liberation is to fight fair.

Chapter Seventy-Six

Work Hard

NEW WORK ETHIC

WORK ISN'T "HARD,"

IF WE LOVE IT.

I was in a zone for a while in the fourth grade. The teacher told my mother, "Randy works hard and plays hard." I liked that. If I was going to have a tombstone, which I am not, I would like to have that written on it. Sometimes I feel like I peaked in the fourth grade.

Speaking of school, I dislike people who get all A's without trying. They are usually the ones who end up being doctors, lawyers, and dentists with big egos. People should be required to try. I feel close to people who try hard, even if it doesn't turn out well—especially if it doesn't turn out well. There is a certain justice in working hard so that we don't have to work hard.

To be fair, there are some aspects of this work-hard idea that need some, well, work. This has to do with backing off and looking at and reflecting on what we are doing. We are so busy making the treadmill go around that we forget what we're doing (getting to financial independence, chapter eighty-three), why we're tired (not living simply, chapter forty-five), how to enjoy the work (bliss, chapter fifty-six), and where we are going (purpose and goals, chapters seventy and seventy-one).

I am glad that there is a strong work ethic in America, so that we all have the opportunity for such a grand life. I get to live in a resort atmosphere and write. If we love our work, do we care if she is liberated? Work isn't "hard" if we love it.

I would like to conclude this chapter with a question regarding our work ethic. How you feel about working hard ina high stress job for two, three, or our decades for the privilege of dying seven to eight years earlier than your mate? This is a scenario in which you create the wealth, and she ends up with it and without you. Or worse, she ends up with the money to spend on her next husban. Your answer to the question may not benefit the titans of commerce with a vested interest in keepinng you on the hamster wheel. Your answer may not benefit our politicians so capable of capturing our vote by spending our hared-earned taxes. Bur your answer could literally be life-giving.

Chapter Seventy-Seven

PLAY HARD

NEW PLAY ETHIC

SO LITTLE TIME

SO MANY GAMES

This may be my favorite chapter in the book. Life is supposed to be fun.

Perhaps I am qualified to write this chapter, since a friend recently referred to me as a "playboy." I suppose that this is because I am a bachelor and have more than a few female friends. I don't know how I can be a real playboy and still have so much heartache over lost love. Aren't playboys supposed to be above this emotional stuff? The truth is I do have a lot of heartache, so perhaps I'm not fully qualified to be a playboy.

On the other hand, I do love to play. I ski, dance, run, walk, bike, backpack, and fly-fish. I attend black tie charity parties. I enjoy fine dining at Burger King. I work out at the gym. I enjoy theater, movies, and concerts. I play tennis, basketball, and blackjack. I have this little boat that goes fast. I went to Hawaii twenty years ago and to Europe thirty years ago. What a guy! Maybe I am qualified to write about "play."

I must confess that I do feel a little guilty about playing so hard. But I don't feel *that* guilty. The ability to play hard has nothing to do with working hard. It does have a lot to do with having time and money. Some people have a lot of money and no time. Other people have a lot of time and no money. Like beauty, you can't have too much time or too much money. The reality is that there are limits; we live life trying to gain maximum benefit from limited resources. On balance, I would prefer having plenty of time to play, while living simply.

As men, we tend to get hung up on playing to win. The XY chromosome seems to be "blessed" with a competitiveness trait. I know; I play to win. The guys playing tennis at the country club have major arguments over line calls and game scores. This sometimes degenerates into unclublike name-calling. Thirty minutes later, over a beer in the clubhouse, we can't remember who won the set, much less the game. There is a lesson in life here. Playing to win is okay. But let's loosen up, laugh, and have fun, too.

I mean, who has time to fool with a liberated woman? Life is short. Play hard.

Chapter Seventy-Eight

Mentor

Getting a mentor can be a good idea. If you want to learn something, go to someone who is doing it, and hopefully doing it well. Having a knowledgeable mentor can be helpful.

A similar idea is appointing your own board of directors. This has to do with more than the fact that you are a business. You need a group of advisors who will help you define dreams, set direction, and achieve goals. I see this as a group of trusted friends on whom you can rely for support and counsel. Ideally, each has particular skills that cover the range of your needs. Having a capable board of advisors can be helpful.

The concept of mentor and advisor becomes counter-productive at a certain point. You are responsible for living your life. If you find someone in your life who has all the answers for you, you need to kill him (figuratively) and get him out of your life. Your life is your expression.

Understanding our collective and divine connection does not require some special power, white-light rebirth, or mountain-top revelation. Enlightenment is not just for Buddha, Christ, Mohammed, or other great spiritual seers. It is available to anyone open to it. You can find your way to becoming Son of God; you are a divine being; heaven is within you. Wisdom is something that you discover for yourself by exploring your heart and soul.

A mate can become as destructive as a mentor. We can get emotionally involved with a women and become consumed in the passion. This seduction feels wonderful. We gain love. And we lose sight of who we are and what we are about.

Seduction can be disguised in ways that are difficult to see at the time. Taken in moderation, a mentor or mate can add diversity and enrichment to life. However, a good thing can go too far and become destructive. You can get lost. Loss of your inner self can have many causes: a babe, a boss, a bottle, or a book.

As a divine being, you may find the truth in yourself.

Chapter Seventy-Nine

MOMMA'S BOY

Whether male or female, we all start life at our mother's breast. The girl stays attached to her mother and her femininity in the process of her growth to becoming adult. As a boy, however, we have a need to separate from Momma and return to achieve our potential as a man.

This separation is unique to men; it's necessary and hurtful. It is necessary because if the attachment is never broken, we continue as "Momma's boy." We never attain the male qualities of aggressiveness and toughness, the "killer" instinct. You have encountered the guy who just can't seem to get out of being the wimp or pussy. This separation usually occurs during our teenage years and accounts for the hell-raising and dangerous behavior of that stage of life. Most guys would prefer not to admit that leaving good old mom is hurtful at a deep level, but it is. To some degree, it wounds the male psyche in a fundamental way.

Some of us separate and never reconnect. We are stuck, one-sided and macho. Some of us reconnect with the wrong things. We get locked on and lost in goods, drugs, gangs, career, sex, gods, and ego. We stay permanently wounded, and become a tragic male figure.

To be whole and achieve our potential as a man, we need to complete the journey and return to the sense of softness, nurturing, and nourishing symbolized by Mother's breast. Being a man is not meant to be a paradox or contradiction between having a "killer" or "pussy" mentality. It is both and something in between. It is a part of our pathway to wholeness to be able to integrate and fully express our masculinity.

This allows us to combine our warrior instinct with our need to nurture and love. This is powerful because we can harness more of our being to achieve our aims. This is enlightening because our aims become more connected and inclusive. We move beyond a macho need to dominate and control the Earth and its creatures, towards something better. We use our full power as men to further the safety and well-being of the Earth community.

Chapter Eighty

WILDMAN

The concept of wildman originates from man's connection to nature. We have come from nature. We have come from a place that is wild, free, beautiful, and dangerous. As a wildman, we have over the ages made our peace with this place. We know, love, and respect it. As a wildman, we long to return to it.

For many years, I have made a personal pilgrimage to the back country of the High Sierra in California. This is the land that naturalist John Muir loved to explore and tried to protect for us. While there, my family, friends and I live in harmony with the land, sky, and water. We brave wild animals and find God in mountain majesty. I rediscover my wildman.

We all relate to our personal wildman in different ways. It could be in backyard meditation, by a pond within a urban park, at a mountain hiking trail, or on a surfboard. If you believe you have found your wildman in a nature program on television, you probably should keep looking, although you are making progress.

Many aspects of our modern society tend to run counter to our wildman. We have the regimentation of our business culture, the white shirt, red tie, and gray flannel suit syndrome. We have the "by the book" control of our regulatory bureaucracy. We have woman's love of wildman and her need to domesticate him. We have the exploitation of our wild and scenic lands to feed our consumer-driven economy, and so on.

Our connection with wildman is important. It allows us to take risks, to find God in the wind and fire, to access our core being through nature, and to loosen up.

Most liberated women I know tend to hunt their men as they run wild in a (preferably five-star) hotel bar, and so be it. I trust that you see the distinction between an authentic wildman and a man running wild.

Chapter Eighty-One

INTEGRATION

As a society, we seem to be hung up on dualistic, black-and-white thinking. One example is the concept of a woman's intuition versus a male's aggressiveness. We have a mother's nurturing versus a father's authoritarianism. A boy gets guns and trucks; a girl gets dolls. These stereotypes are comforting; they give us a set of expectations on how to behave. The woman is soft. The man is tough and hard. As a man, we want to be accepted and to act like a man.

This thinking is limiting. The qualities mentioned in the preceding paragraph are all part of the human experience, not exclusively male or female. In fact, they are better understood as personality types of either sex. Do you know a woman who seeks power and is aggressive? Have you ever met a man who is sensitive and feeling? Perhaps he is the fun-seeking, life-of-the-party type. She tends to be the quiet, contemplative seeker of peace and tranquillity. These are various personality traits that we all possess to one degree or another; they are not based on gender. A man or woman can express power, sensitivity, fun or peace. Giving a man a set of one-dimensional, supposedly male qualities such as being strong, rugged, aggressive, and tough stifles the full development of personality.

Part of the confusion in understanding what it is to be a man relates to this outdated role model. We men are finding clarity in what it means to be a man. We are moving to a new, improved masculine role model that is multidimensional. Men are embracing the notion that by developing qualities such as intuition, caring, and loving, we can develop more fully as human beings and enjoy a richer life. We are taking two seemingly opposite ways of being (hard and soft) and integrating them into a better way. It takes practice, but it can be done.

The beauty of this is that we are freed to be all that we can be—a loving warrior. Perhaps this can be a part of man's answer to woman's liberation. She's liberated; you're integrated.

If it hurts, if you're sad, and if you feel like crying, then cry. You'll feel better. You are a man, and real men can cry.

P.S. Why is the macho guy talking to his horse? Because he has been too long without a woman or with the wrong woman and needs to read *The Man's Book.*

Chapter Eighty-Two

THE KING AND I

My astrological sign is Leo, the Lion. My male ego likes to think of Leo as king of the jungle. The concept of "king" is religious, as in "King of the Jews." We have many legendary, historical figures who were powerful, if not enlightened, kings—King Henry VIII or King Richard the Lionhearted, for example. We crowned our modern-day rock star "the King." A man's house is his castle, and in it, he is king. I love the idea of king. This archetype is buried deep in the male psyche.

The patriarchal king in our society is dead. He has been murdered with malice aforethought by woman. You see, the king has headed a patriarchal system throughout recorded history. The king has ruled the realm, and in so doing has controlled and dominated woman. Over the past two or three decades in America and beyond, woman has rebelled and killed the king. She got a job, a divorce, and the kids, and has become liberated from male domination. The queen is delighted. Long live the queen!

Is there any wonder that the male psyche is damaged and confused? When will this rebellion and the carnage end? What will it take for man to redefine his role and heal his wounded psyche?Can man be educated to grasp the difference between domination and leadership?

Being a patriarchal king was a big burden, especially since the queen was never happy with it. Getting release from the burden is painful initially as we mourn the loss of our patriarchal position of "privilege." The loss, however, becomes a blessing in time, as man discovers the real king. The loss creates a need to start over and redefine the areas of man's fulfillment. We do this by opening a communicative process with God through our soul.

Hopefully, we find comfort in our being (in our divine being. Hopefully, this brings the enlightenment required to lead the dance of life, not control her. We may find help in sharing our pain and discoveries with others. We may receive insights from friends, society, religion, goddess, or possibly this book. However, ultimately this is an inner journey, and we will find the true king *within*. I trust that ultimately we will discover a king with whom we are at peace and with whom we are in love; the fruits of the search will allow us to express our kingly manhood in new and better ways. Long live the king!

Chapter Eighty-Three

Financial Independence

RANDY'S RULE #1:

THE MEASURE OF SUCCESS IS FREEDOM.

After your mate exits, your parents die, your children leave, your pet departs, and your health fails, what do you have? You have your soul and your wallet. Hopefully you have put something in them—your spirit and your checkbook—to sustain you.

Women seem to appreciate men who achieve financial independence. Many women, however, don't seem to appreciate the process of getting there. They see the problem as how much you make, not how much they spend at the mall. We men like to rank women by their hip-to-waist ratio (not bust-to-hip ratio). Studies have been done on this; it has to do with a presumption of fertility. And women like to rank men according to our net worth and our capacity to provide for them. Your ability to achieve financial independence will influence your success with females. We want hip-to-waist ratio; females want security. This may be a harsh simplification, but it's often the reality.

Your government, employer, mate, or offspring will not get you to financial independence. You will be the one who gets you to financial independence. Having gotten there, you will get to do what you want to do, when you want to do it. This is a good thing; it needs to be set as a goal in your consciousness. You can do it if you try.

There are three primary things that you will need to do to achieve financial independence.

First, you will establish a value system of living simply so that you keep your expenses at a reasonable level (please review chapter forty-five).

Second, you will "pay yourself first," perhaps 10 percent of your monthly income, into an investment account.

And third, you will periodically review your account, keeping funds invested in high-growth securities, such as stocks or no-load mutual funds. You will be financially independent when the growth and income from the investment account exceeds your expenses on an ongoing basis.

When you have arrived at financial independence, you will discover that the goal of the journey was not to maximize money. The basic purpose of financial independence is to achieve the freedom to find your soul. You will find the opportunity to explore love of self, nurture significant relationships, pursue your bliss, and build community.

If I had to choose, this may be the single most important way to survive women's liberation.

Chapter Eighty-Four

Just Dying To Live

LIFE IS A BITCH
AND THEN SHE HAD PUPPIES

IF LIFE IS A BITCH
IT BEATS THE ALTERNATIVE

I am not an expert on dying. When I get to be knowledgeable on the subject, I won't be around to comment on the experience. But I have seen people die. I watched my father pass away. He had lung cancer from cigarettes that are "not addictive." He was conscious when he died, and just slipped away. I was in Vietnam, where I watched an "enemy" guy die. It was war. He would probably be alive today had we not killed him. Death is not pretty.

This may sound morbid, but death is something to fully contemplate. I think that coming to terms with our mortality as men is helpful for several reasons.

First, we come to an appreciation of our limited and precious time here. Going to war and cheating death did that for me. Facing death straight up creates an appreciation for just being, regardless of our circumstances. It also gives us an opportunity to reflect on what we want from life.

Another reason to look forward to death has to do with fear. People live life with a sense of foreboding that they are going to get hurt or ill, and die. The trick is to blast through the fear by confronting it. It is going to get us sooner or later anyway, so why worry?

A third reason to contemplate death is to use it to understand the meaning of life and its relationship to what happens, if anything, after death. Without dealing with the idea of death, we never get to the concept of the hereafter and the spirit life.

A final reason is preparation. This means living our life in a way that is tidy, without leaving too many loose ends for other people to clean up, just in case something happens unexpectedly.

Liberation seems quite insignificant when taken in perspective with this stuff. Let's leave the whining to the libbers and get on with life while we still have it.

Did you hear about the old guy who died in the midst of making love with his cute young girlfriend? He came and went at the same time! This gives new meaning to death giving life its deepest reality.

Chapter Eighty-Five

BUSINESSMAN

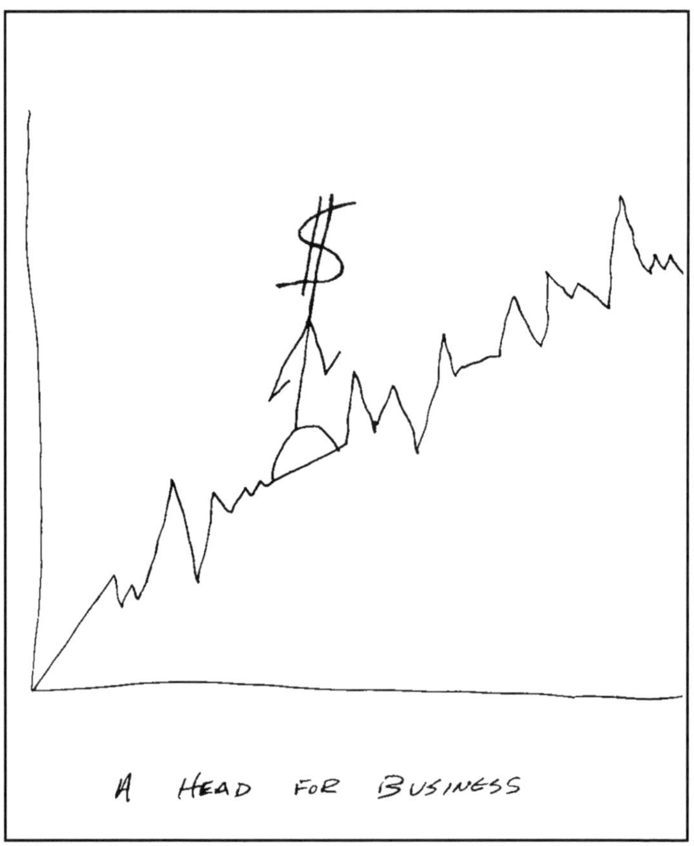

Business is the monetary, modern-day equivalent of survival of the fittest. The businessman is perhaps the primary archetype for the contemporary male. We are all in business. The employee sells his time and skill to his company. The minister provides his spiritual services to his congregation. The actor markets his performance talent within his "non-profit" theater group. The proprietor offers goods or services to his customers. These are all examples of the same thing: an individual in business.

I know this. I have been a manager of a large corporation, a president of a small corporation, a sole proprietor of my own company, and a president, director, or officer of three non-profit organizations. I have a master's degree in business administration from a major university. Fundamentally, all business is the same. It is an individual or organization that has revenues, expenses, and, hopefully, a positive and growing bottom line. You, as a man, have revenues, expenses, and a bottom line.

The trouble with business is that you may be subject to producing profits in circumstances that are out of your control. This is especially true today. At one time, there was an element of paternalism in corporate America. If you did a good job, you got to keep it. At present, corporations have a single-minded, short-term focus on maximizing shareholder benefit. As an employee, this means that you are subject to downsizing and outsourcing at any time. As president or stock boy, you ultimately serve at the pleasure and whim of the board of directors. The proprietor must continually satisfy the ever-changing tastes of his customers; otherwise, he is on to his next venture. If the minister's spiritual followers didn't like his last message, their weekly donations will move to the church around the corner. And so it goes. Business is tricky, tough, and unforgiving.

Business can be fun; it's the high of closing the deal. Business can be rewarding; it's the camaraderie of working with a team to get something profitably accomplished.

I suggest that you live simply, and use business for as long as necessary to achieve financial independence. This eventually provides control of your life so that you can do whatever you damn well please. This is a survival technique, because independent women respect independent men.

Chapter Eighty-Six

WOMAN AS LIFE, MAN AS SLAVE

IF I WANTED A BITCH,
I'D GET A DOG

Woman is life. Man protects woman. This is such a sweet sentiment. It is powerful; it is buried deep in both the male and female psyche. It has functioned for thousands of years to advance the human species. In ancient times, it saved the pregnant female from being eaten by lions and tigers.

It has "progressed" through the ages to give females a place of privilege and preference in virtually all areas of modern society. Here are a few examples:

By custom, a man has the responsibility to initiate contact with a woman. The woman has the right to send the man to jail if she doesn't like the way he did it. Her kisses and caresses said "yes," but in the morning she decided she meant "no." The man is "guilty," but where is her responsibility?

The government has given women the option of going into combat; men have the obligation. There are 58,183 names of men on the Vietnam War Memorial; only 8 names belong to women.

For the same offenses (rape, aggravated assault, burglary, and larceny), the courts give men from 59 to 75 percent longer sentences than women.

The government funds a safety net for females with children, but not for men with children. It is called "aid to 'families' with dependent children," and the family is required or forced to be fatherless.

The female has the right to decide if she wants to keep the child. The man has no such choice, but he does have the obligation to pay for the child for eighteen years.

Sexual initiatives by men are the most frequent type of "harassment" of females in the workplace. When successful, it is called "courtship"; when unsuccessful, it is called "sexual harassment." Why are females not prosecuted for using their sexuality for workplace advancement?

Men have the responsibility to provide. This often results in working outside the home in stressful or dangerous jobs that cause us to live on average almost *eight years less* than females. If what he provides isn't enough for her, she has the right to have the divorce court make him legally obligated to pay. If he doesn't like it, he can express his displeasure from jail. Why isn't the female responsible for financial support, with the man given the option of providing in-home child care?

Today, this system of female privileges has outlived its usefulness. In a modern society, lions do not eat helpless females. Women do not need protection. Children need protection. Men and women now need to take equal responsibility, both financially and emotionally, for the upbringing of their children. Men need to value themselves enough to overthrow their role as slave. Men are created equal. Until men live as long as women in our society, we are not equal.

Chapter Eighty-Seven

An Apple a Day

It's not much fun being a man when you are sick and feeling like hell.

There is more to a healthy body than a bag of apples and your friendly health care professional. There is also what you feed your spirit and mind.

When we ask God for direction and live in harmony with our soulfulness, we will be much happier. When we use our soul to guide a positive mental attitude, we discover the healing connection between spirit, mind, and body. Your spirit and mind are the cause; you body is the effect. Said another way, a relationship with soul generates a peace of mind that allows the body to function in a relaxed way. This spirit-mind-body connection tends to be circular; when we feel good physically, it is easier to feed soul and build mind.

We should all envision an active, healthy life past one hundred years of age. We can be assisted in getting there by creating the expectation that this will happen. If you think it can happen, you can at least improve the chances. There are small social systems in which people typically live past one hundred years of age. They eat unprocessed, simple foods. They live an active, simple life. They expect to live past one hundred, and they do live past one hundred. Let's contrast this with a high-stress job that we hate, allowing us to live a fast-lane life that we hate? What usually happens?

After we get the spiritual and mental stuff right, it is important that we eat a balanced diet and get regular exercise.

Most guys will agree to go to the doctor only if mortally wounded. Modern medicine can produce extraordinary results. If you don't feel good, don't suffer like a "man." Go see the doctor and ask questions.

These two guys are contemplating what they would do if their doctor told them they had only three months to live. The one guy says, "Well, I would update my will, say 'good-bye' to my family, and book a trip to Tahiti with a beautiful redhead."

The other guy says, "I'd change doctors."

Chapter Eighty-Eight

Renaissance Man, Reborn

The Renaissance (A.D. 1400 to 1700) marked the transition from medieval to modern times, and is characterized by the rebirth of art, literature, and learning. In modern vernacular, a renaissance man is a person of diversity and multiplicity; he is a master of many disciplines. A historical transition to a time of greater enlightenment and to a symbol of man that is multifaceted is a perfect analogy for the type of man I am trying to suggest here. Like a diamond, the man with many facets reflects the light of life with great brilliance.

The renaissance man of old was able to write a poem, play a tune, fight a duel, love his woman, and converse in several languages about the political and scientific ideas of the day. He was a writer, a musician, a lover, a warrior, a statesman, and a scientist.

If you go to a party and have an encounter with a stranger, the question is "What do you do?" We tend to be defined by our job, and more specifically, by our specialization within our profession. I am a mortgage broker, and you are an ear, nose, and throat specialist. But is this who we really are? I don't think so.

The renaissance man of today defines himself by more than his job. He is warrior, trickster, businessman, wildman, and king. His intellectual curiosity covers the letters, arts, and sciences/technology. He gives himself the freedom to express his love, fierceness, compassion, and strength. He nurtures his self and his soul, so as to find full expression of his bliss. He can hold his wife's hand in the delivery room, hold his own in a tennis match, hold a conference with his church group, and hold out for an Earth-friendly solution. The renaissance man is multi-dimensional.

This doesn't replace the old concept of the renaissance man, but builds on it. It revives the rich heritage of our ancient history and mythology. It embraces a wider range of spiritual values (e.g., love-giver) and personality traits (e.g., power-seeker) that enhance the richness of our lives. It seeks to integrate and connect seemingly paradoxical qualities, such as toughness and intuition, into a more satisfying and fuller life expression. And by doing so, we arrive at a new renaissance man.

Chapter Eighty-Nine

TAKE ME TO YOUR . . .

The genius of a man in a relationship is to define a vision of what the relationship should, could, or might be—a dream to which both the man and woman aspire. He then stays focused on keeping both people moving toward the vision. This is leadership, and it can be a powerful force for uplifting and binding a relationship.

Feminists have done great harm in their attempt to extinguish man's fire, his role as leader. It's one thing for women to kill paternalism and domination; please see chapter 82, The King and I. It's tragic for women to emasculate the man's ability to lead, because in the process they emasculate his masculinity. A man and a woman, literally and figuratively, dance through life. Somehow the relationship works better if someone leads the dance. If a woman compliments a man's place of leadership in their relationship, he is in a much stronger place to affirm her self-sufficiency and her femininity.

This differs from a traditional powerpoint relationship in which the man wields ultimate control because he makes the money. This differs from a fifty-fifty partnership of equals in which no one has control, there is constant jockeying for control, and the relationship is often drifting out of control. Yes, you can exercise leadership in a powerpoint and partnership relationship. But this is seldom the case because of the control issues that arise.

Leadership is the process of setting a direction so that you (plural) are moving on the same pathway toward the same purpose. This is a dialogue, but it requires someone to call the meeting and set the agenda. The person who does this will have some significant influence on what gets discussed and on the outcome. This sets the stage for participating in a process of coming to agreement on the vision or purpose of the relationship, and how to get there. The best leader can inspire the follower(s) to a higher purpose and then help them get there.

A leader may have a measure of power and control. But the process of enlightened leadership has nothing to do with maintaining or using power and control. Leadership is simply a process. The female is always free to exercise her prerogative to vote with her feet and be liberated from her "leader."

With a little luck, perhaps you can talk to her about something other than the local gossip. Can you define with her the structure of the relationship?

Play—How will we have fun?

Space—Where will we be?

Time—When will we be together?

Money—Who will pay for what?

With a little leadership, perhaps, together you can create a dream.

This guy is proudly describing his relationship to a buddy. He says, "I make all the big decisions."

His friend asks, "So what kind of big decisions do you make?"

The guy ponders this for a moment, and says, "I don't know; they haven't come up yet."

Chapter Ninety

Penis Envy

Have you ever been nagged by a female? Every ninety days or so, she seems to have a biological need to present you with her List. If she was living with Jesus Christ Himself, she would find some issues for the List. Why did you have all those baskets of loaves and fishes left over when you fed the multitudes? That was wasteful. Why didn't you make the good wine sooner, so those nice people wouldn't have been embarrassed at the wedding feast? That was inconsiderate. What in God's name is wrong with you? I don't intend for this to be a sacrilegious example, but you get the idea. Females have a reputation for nagging. I ask you, is the reputation well-founded? Is there a reason why Jesus remained a bachelor?

I have something more than a theory about this. God really did give women the short end of the stick, so to speak. I don't know any man who would want to come back in the next life as a female. Lots of women believe that we men have the better deal; they would prefer to try it our way next time. I know this beyond anecdotal experience; surveys have actually been done on this subject. More women would prefer to be men than the reverse.

I can only speculate on why this is, but there are some fairly obvious reasons. Have you ever been in the delivery room and watched a baby being born? For months, they prepare us for this, and it's still painful just to watch. Females have this complicated biological plumbing that provides a somewhat messy and uncomfortable monthly reminder that it's there. In contrast, we have this handy thing that we can use in the woods by simply stepping behind a tree. Female mood swings have been compared to a "wave," but the guy who came up with that was being nice. Bungee jumping would be a better comparison. It can be exciting to watch, but dangerous if you get too close when she is doing it. We run faster, jump higher, and throw the ball farther. I believe that, deep down, females understand that they have some basic disadvantages. It is why women envy men.

Please be compassionate with her; it's not easy being a woman. Please read on.

Chapter Ninety-One

MACHO MAN EXPOSED

If you are feeling smug about how wonderful it is to be a man, you might consider a few facts. Women outlive men by an average of almost eight years, and the gap is increasing. By a wide margin, men are more likely than women to commit crimes, go to jail, and be victimized. More men than women succeed in committing suicide. Men may prefer to be men.

Women may have penis envy. However, the truth is that being a man can be hazardous to your health.

The central cause of these disadvantages is that men live lives that are less healthy than women; this is not due to the superior biology of females. There are several reasons that do account for it.

1) Society tells boys to be manly. The role model for "manly" is often a dad who is absent, physically or emotionally. He is out slaying dragons, killing lions, swimming with sharks and/or waging war on the neighboring tribe or corporation. Or he is around the household as the enforcer. Men often grow into adult life without an example of a male who is accessible, loving, and caring. By default, the mother trains the boy in the unhealthy role of serving the goddess.

2) Society defines manhood as being tough and strong. We are supposed to play hurt. Only sissies go to the doctor. "Real men" don't cry and express feelings. Men are trained to live lives that are emotionally disconnected from themselves. We are out of touch with our physical and emotional pain, and with our true inner self.

3) Our culture is defined by materialism and growth. A man's worth to many females is judged by his net worth and by his employment success. The stress and pressure of this one-dimensional lifestyle makes men prone to mental and physical breakdown. By the time we crash, the lesson is learned too late.

4) Assisted by our hormonal imperative and social expectations, men buy into the myth of serving the goddess. Sooner or later, we discover the reality of the goddess, with her rules, lists, and prerogatives. This discovery can be emotionally, financially, and physically damaging.

The lesson is simple. We need to slow down and get in touch with our true inner self. The freedom to be aligned with our true inner self is the ultimate measure of success. The measuring stick for equality is when men live as long as women.

P.S. Why does the macho guy beg for sex? Because he is thinking with his penis, and needs to read *The Man's Book*.

Chapter Ninety-Two

Getting to We

I was reading about a couple who recently celebrated their fiftieth wedding anniversary. The reporter who interviewed them for the newspaper article asked them to reveal their secret for a successful marriage. Their secret was simple. They said that they lived life as a "we."

With childhood abuse or relationship traumas, we tend to get closed and protective and hard. We put up the hard shell, like a tortoise, and stick out our head very carefully—and only when necessary. We survive on lettuce and if someone actually gets close, they get snapped at. This is a lousy way to live.

The problem with liberation is that it creates a "me" mentality. My hope is that women can develop their independence as a self-sufficiency, not as separateness. This self-sufficiency gives a woman a wonderful sense of being able to take care of herself. This expands her power in the relationship so that she has leverage with her man beyond her beauty and charm. She no longer needs to demean herself by withholding and bartering her sexuality in the relationship. She brings her whole self to a man, not so much to have financial needs met, but to be more fully actualized and expressed.

Similarly, my hope is that men can develop their independence in the direction of wholeness. Men need to embrace parts of themselves that are usually considered female. Did we win our woman based on our ability to be tough, controlling, and successful? The man's role of powermonger and money provider comes at a huge price. We wake up one day and discover that we have lost touch with our soft, imperfect, and human self. In the process, we may have lost touch with her as well. We, as men, need to develop our ability to communicate feelings, be intuitive, and foster nurturing. These traits, usually associated with the female personality, can add balance and wholeness to our masculinity. This will also give us the ability to be more sensitive and effective in leadership of our personal relationships and group involvement.

The blending of two self-sufficient, whole human beings by giving to "we" is powerful and exciting. The love equation is not one-half plus one-half equals one. It's one plus one equals infinity.

Chapter Ninety-Three

Down, But Not Out

To a man we are in need of healing. Being the strongest, toughest, baddest, richest, smartest guy on the block in order to win and keep our woman has taken its toll. We have world leaders who brutalize their people. We have captains of industry who downsize their employees and lie to their customers. And we have evangelists who sin. I know I had to get a closet organizer to handle all my skeletons. If you are into drugs, sickness, gangs, crime, or poverty, you are a wounded man. We are all broken to some degree. Falling or getting off the pedestal is good for three reasons.

First, we need to understand that it is okay for us to be broken. This runs counter to the strongest, toughest, baddest, richest, smartest fallacy that we pretend to live. Don't you hate living with the pretension that everything is okay, when it isn't? The low-grade or high-grade pain that you feel is trying to tell you that you are broken, and what to fix. Rather than suck up the pain "like a man" and pretend that we are some kind of macho machine, we need to take the time to get in touch with our feelings. If you are experiencing it, someone else has felt it. There is some comfort in knowing that you are not alone in your hurt. When we admit that we are broken, we can face the hurt and begin to heal.

Second, our wound can further our compassion for others. Isn't it amazing how, with a life reversal, ego is lost and humility gained? Isn't it interesting how we tend to be a little more understanding of people who are experiencing similar reversals? He who has not sinned gets to cast the first stone. It is surprising to notice the number of stones that are cast daily in our society by presumably perfect human beings.

One example is the talk-show psychologists. They are constantly telling the great unwashed just how dirty they are. Their book jackets portray them in loving relationships as part of functional families. The truth is that they are broken just like the rest of us. They provide sound-bite solutions based on thirty second "evaluations" of complex beings. They advise that you get "healthy" by walking out on your "unhealthy" mate. What they tend to forget is that both people are broken to a degree and probably deserve and need each other. The challenge is to have compassion for your mate and fix yourself *within* the relationship.

Third, our pain gives us a wake-up call to find insights about our divine nature. We find *love* as the way to heal our wounds and move us to a new and better place. The "fall," symbol of painful life struggles, is necessary for a resurrection of self as a divine, loving being.

Chapter Ninety-Four

DECEPTION AND COQUETRY

Some females enjoy being chased, wooed, and courted. They never reveal the truth—that they wish to be caught. They believe that it's coy to play a bit dumb. They go to singles bars with their friends to talk and are in complete denial that they are there to meet men. They reward our generosity with self-serving and often false flattery. They tease us with a flash of leg here, a wry glance there. They are embarrassed or surprised when we look at them. They give us a hint that they are interested and then deny that it was a hint.

They endure suction, tuck, implant, and reduction in the pursuit of vanity. They are offended at any suggestion that this is for the purpose of being more seductive. They purchase millions of steamy romance novels but would never admit their real-life desires. They give us the half-truth now and the full truth when and if it suits them. Their assortment of lip glosses, eye shadows, and nail polishes encompass a broader spectrum of colors than the pigments on Van Gogh's palette.

They wish to be as attractive as possible and must always play hard to get. They purchase the most alluring perfume and negligee. They can share their desires with a girlfriend, but they must never admit to a man that they really want sex. A woman doesn't understand how she can get you to value her or the sex if she gives it away for free. How can she get you to pay for it if she actually admitted to liking it? The coquetry serves her purpose.

Some women have the idea that they need to practice deception in order to ensnare men. Females are constantly creating and changing certain rules of engagement for this deception, under the pretense that "all's fair." Is all fair in love and war? The rules are necessary and effective for some females—for a while. Eventually, however, we will find them out. One day we wake up to her with makeup off and soul bared, and we ask, "Who is this anyway?"

Women believe that men are supposed to love this nonsense. To the contrary, it smacks of game playing at best and dishonesty at worst. If you put up with it, you will suffer in the end. And the standard of acceptable female behavior will be lowered so that we will all suffer. Don't lower yourself to her level and get confused and frustrated by her female foolishness. Keep yourself focused on what you want. I believe we are easy to please. Men appreciate beautiful women who enjoy expressing their love for us in straightforward, sincere, and sexual ways.

There is a simple, direct way to cut through her stuff. If you love her, I suggest that you tell her and ask two questions: Do you love me? Will you make love with me?

Chapter Ninety-Five

FEMINISM

The women's movement is a collection of people, organizations, and ideas. Some of it is helpful to men, and some of it is destructive and polarizing. In any event, the feminist agenda is diverse. It includes parity with men in the workplace, the Equal Rights Amendment, affirmative action, the right of women to choose an abortion, a national day-care program, and penalties for male failure to support children.

Females have lived and thrived under the traditional view of manhood, to protect and provide, for a long time. Over the ages, women have socialized men to serve the goddess. This by extension has created the princess syndrome. Man has harnessed himself to the treadmill to serve his woman. If you don't, the divorce court provides her with the assurance that she will reap half or more of the spoils. As men, we have been victimized by this one-dimensional, sole-provider approach to being a man.

Many females find this paternalistic system to be controlling and therefore unacceptable. Other females don't appreciate this, as they like the old way. Men ask: "So what is it going to be ladies? Do you wish to be treated like a queen? Or do you want equal rights in the work place and to become self-sufficient?" And women reply: "Yes!" Is it any wonder that men are having difficulty dealing with this?

The more enlightened women have evolved to something better. These women have rejected the notion that their place is to trade their beauty and sex for security. They have openly relieved some of the pressure of being a provider from their men. They have found other, constructive ways to express their being and to make a positive impact in society and in their relationships. These women rightfully revel in their self-sufficiency at the side of their man.

A potential danger for men is to respond to the many destructive aspects of feminism. For example, the liberated feminists blame men for our perceived domination and control of women dating back to Adam and Eve. I'll take responsibility for my behavior, but I won't take a guilt trip over what some Neanderthal man may have done. Feminists' dismantling of paternalism has confused most men. Are we leaders or partners or cast-offs? Men need to update their leadership skills to evoke participation rather than impose control. As such, we need to stop apologizing for taking our seat at the head of the table. Another destructive feminist view is that the nature of man is to rape, pillage and plunder. Men aren't the only ones capable of violence. The exercise of power in a destructive way is a human tendency that is not exclusive to men. And finally, the feminist tries to achieve her goals from a position that is separate from and opposed to man. Her approach is counterproductive because it is confrontational. If we all work together, then we can all move forward to a better and higher plane.

P.S. How do amoebae and libbers make love? The don't; they aren't sufficiently evolved.

Chapter Ninety-Six

THE MEN'S MOVEMENT

Without the women's movement, there would be no men's movement. We would have just blindly continued, trapped and harnessed on the treadmill. Women have pushed for independence and liberation, and the men's movement has responded. That is, if no response is a response. The battle of the sexes has been a war in which men have mostly stayed in their foxholes.

Like feminists, the men's movement is a collection of movements. Each is in a political and social struggle to define itself and its relationship with or against women.

The *conservative* belief is that man's responsibility is to protect and provide for woman. This is legitimized by man's and civilization's dominance over the natural world. The conservatives are opposed to feminism and long for the good old days of Ozzie and Harriet when women stayed at home with the babies.

The *pro-feminists* hold that manhood and paternalism are maintained by man's hatred of and violence toward women. Men and women are limited by the traditional male role. To combat sexism, both male and female, men need to become more giving caretakers and more fully human. Men need to debunk the macho-man myth. Men need to discover the "integration" of the full range of their personality.

The *men's rights* perspective is that men have been victimized by the traditional male role. The feminist movement has worsened the situation with expanded women's rights and male-bashing. The men's rights agenda seeks to redress laws in the areas of divorce and child custody, among other things.

The *psycho/spiritual* belief is that masculinity is based on our deep subconscious and on our connection with the spirit world. This is observed by understanding ancient mythology and ritual and carrying that knowledge into modern-day thought. Women have historically shown better intuitive power to touch their inner being. Man needs to explore and connect with his spirituality, from the development of his sixth sense to an embrace of his dark side. Man needs to reach into mythological archetypes such as funnyman, king, wildman, and renaissance man in order to find his true inner self.

My bias is to integrate aspects of the men's movement that bond with feminism in positive ways, and thus affirm and advance masculinity. Hopefully, men and women will benefit as a result.

It's more fun to love them than to fight them.

Chapter Ninety-Seven

THE SYNERGY OF THE SEXES

Both the women's and men's movements will benefit by finding common ground and by jointly working to affirm the areas of agreement. This can generate a synergy in which we can accomplish more working together than working apart.

One area of synergy is that men and women both seek a more diverse expression of their respective roles. Women are looking to be productive and fairly treated members of the economic system, released from male domination in the home. Men are looking to find a fuller and richer life detached from the harness. This includes a better development of man's spiritual connection, family responsibilities, and community involvement. Perhaps most importantly, this has given us the opportunity to slow down and become more in tune with our inner self. The demise of the role of the sole provider removes the pressure to produce and gives men more options.

Another area ripe for synergy has to do with men being more verbal and women being more physical. Women are asking men to be more verbally expressive and emotionally connected to them. Do you enjoy sharing conversation and expressing feelings with the woman you love? Men can do this. Men want women to be more physically connected both in sex and in play. Empowered women make love as an expression of love and don't need to use their body as a tool to get what they want. There are women who enjoy sex for the joy and pleasure of it, without a hidden agenda. If you want her to be more physically playful, try taking her on a hike. You can actually walk and talk at the same time. She'll like that. And hopefully you will have enough energy to get really physical when you return. You'll like that.

Finding common ground or mutuality within the movements will be more productive than bitching about our victimization or fighting women. Some issues may need to be resolved by the lawyers in the courts and by the politicians in the legislature. But perhaps we would do better to find more of the synergy together in the bedroom.

How do porcupines make love? Skillfully.

Chapter Ninety-Eight

Person Specific

DEAR MS. P.S.,

BELIEVE IN MIRACLES.

I LOVE YOU.

____

MAN*

* AFTER READING THE MAN'S BOOK

This book has defined stereotypes of female behaviors. The concept of the liberated woman has been described as one such stereotype. A straw woman was created and arrows were shot figuratively through her. I make no apology for these generalizations, because they have helped us understand the way some females think and act. And I make no apology for shooting the arrows, because the liberated woman needed to die. The liberated woman, alienated and separated from man, needed to pass on, just as the macho, paternalistic, dominating male needed to be killed. These stereotypes can help us see and be sensitive to trends and tendencies, so that we avoid getting blindsided by them in real life. There is no condemnation of women intended here. I love women. This book exposes certain female behaviors exhibited by some females. My intention is to provide helpful ways of dealing with them.

While stereotypes can be helpful to our thinking, they are what they are—generalizations. Sometimes people fit the mold and sometimes they don't. Not every woman is liberated. Not every woman seeks to be a princess. Not every woman has rules, lists, a nagging nature, or a fickle character. The danger is that we come to deal with all people as stereotypes and not as dynamic individuals. Character traits are specific to each person.

There is an element of fate and luck in connecting with this specific person. You may find her at seventeen or eighteen years of age, or she may appear in your life at seventy-seven or eighty-eight. The timing is not entirely in our control; it is God-given.

We can, however, improve the odds by working with God and getting ourselves right with life. We do that by maintaining a positive vision or dream. Our belief system will become manifest in our life. If we feed ourselves with positive thinking about women, that is what we will get—eventually. The chances are that she will appear in our life. Or, she and you may achieve a certain enlightenment and change in ways that will cause you to discover that she was in your life all the time. Isn't she wonderful?

There is one important insight about finding her or realizing that you have already found her. She isn't perfect! At times she may be a royal pain in the ass. If you love her unconditionally, she may on occasion love you. That's typical.

You can elevate your vision to the extraordinarily untypical. Some women illuminate life with a beauty that runs deep. They are independently loyal, elegantly frugal, unpretentiously sophisticated, sensuously loving, and compassionately sincere. Loving and being loved by such a woman is every man's dream. She may not be a goddess, but being with her can be heavenly. Believe in miracles.

Chapter Ninety-Nine

ANGER

GET OVER IT!

"Bile" is a pejorative word that describes anger with a negative connotation. A lady friend called me today and expressed her hope that I wasn't putting too much bile into this book. I am afraid that she will be disappointed. In fact, I would like to encourage men to see clearly what is happening to them and get damn mad about it.

Women don't want us to get pissed off because in a way they like the status quo. They like having a job and at the same time getting their meal ticket punched by a man on Saturday night. They like the freedom to file for primary custody of the children and to have a man legally obligated to pay for it. They like to use their "poor me" dependency to control us. They like the feeling of walking away from a relationship at any time for any reason and of having doors opened for them. They like leading us around by our (you know) nose so that we will follow their rules. So when men react negatively to female fickleness, foolishness, and flightiness, women would describe it as "bile."

I prefer to describe it as righteous indignation. When you own the moral high ground, it is perfectly all right to be angry. It's what Christ felt and acted on when he drove the money changers from the temple. The next time you are violated by her nonsense, it is most appropriate to feel your anger. You want to make sure that it is not only felt, but expressed in a reasoned and reasonable manner. Your anger is something to respect as a powerful force for your inner change. It is an important source of insight and healing. Learn from your anger.

I hope that there are areas in this book that lead you to a place of constructive anger and a resolve that you are just not going to accept her mush any more. Recognize and seek to move away rom her negativity and nonsense Most importantly, I hope that you find some positive suggestions for moving yourself, your life, and your relationships to a higher level.

How can you stay angry with a species that can cancel a date or serve you with divorce papers one week, and in the next week fix you up with a great piece of banana cream pie? Staying bitter with women is counterproductive. Just ask her to give you a great . . . (use your imagination). Forgiveness is a virtue.

Chapter One Hundred

Macho Revisited

There are men, and there are a lot of macho guys trying to be men. Here are a dozen examples:

GUY	versus	**MAN**
Smokes on Horse		Gets Fit
Eats Nails		Eats Well
Loves Cockfights		Loves Women
Drives Hard		Gets There
Loves to Philander		Loves to Father
Dominates		Leads
Gets High		Gets Better
Makes War		Makes Love & Peace
Collects Toys		Lives Fully & Simply
Makes Big Money		Makes Big Difference
Sends Junk Mail		Saves Forests
Serves Princess		Is Own Man

Masculinity is not about being a lewd-talking, hard-driving warmonger, with the goal of collecting the most toys and/or making the most money. It is not about catering to the goddess or being soft and defined by her rules and prerogatives. Masculinity is more than getting a piece of a rock and a piece of ass.

Being a man is about character and values. It is the toughness required to be loving, nurturing, protecting, forgiving, and compassionate. It is the strength necessary to do what you say you are going to do. It is the courage to stand up for the highest truth. It is the creative leadership necessary to move your relationship and your community to the next level. It is finding harmony with the Earth and with the feminine. You know who you are and what you are about, and it feels damn good.

I trust that you can see how this relates to women's liberation and other female nonsense. Liberation is irrelevant, because she has chosen to be separated from man. Her rules, lists, and prerogatives are irrelevant, because you have a higher and better standard. You are in a place of self-respect, proud to be a man.

The one hundredth way to survive women's liberation is to celebrate being a man.

Chapter One Hundred One

YOUR WAY

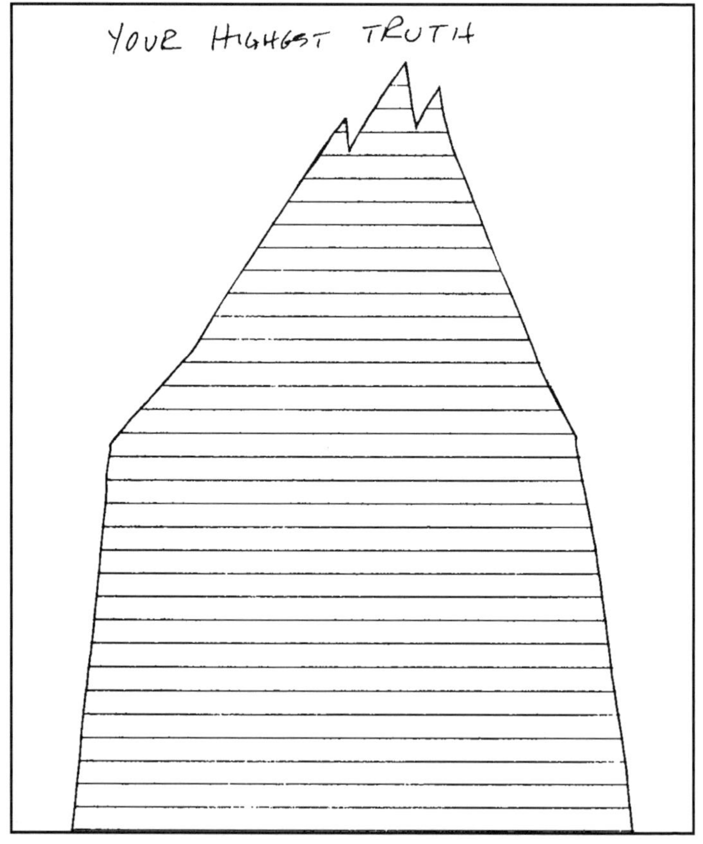

It is your life, and when it is over you will want to say, "I did it my way. I took the hits and had the courage to do it this way." This will hopefully be your way of using your special gifts to fully express your divine nature as a child of God, and to follow His purpose for your life.

I would like to close with how I began. In the foreword, I expressed the idea that "the final word will be your own." This means that you may take some of my thoughts and combine them with your own unique creativity to achieve your way. Please take a few minutes and jot down some ideas on how you will make *The Man's Book* work for you.

So, the one hundred and first way to survive women's liberation and other female nonsense is mostly blank, inviting your expression. Good luck.

Do more of the things I LOVE to do:
hiking in the Back Country
Riding my bike
Swimming in the Ocean -
Being at the Beach
Hanging out w/ friends
Increase my self-confidence/raise my self-esteem.
Work out more consistently.
Do not be dependent on family.
Integrate spiritual path into my life.
Set up computer/get on line!

Postscript

For Her Eyes Only

My message for any women reading this book is "Viva your femininity (see chapter one) and your independence (see chapter three)." Your challenge is to create enough financial independence so as to avoid the sacrifice of your love for an economic safety net. Your self-sufficiency has released us from the bondage of being your sole provider. You have thus helped to set men free so they can find a richer and expanded sense of our masculinity. We can now explore our connection with you, the children, the community, and the self in new, diverse ways. We thank you.

My message for the liberated woman is that you have made your point. Over the past twenty-five years, you have succeeded in killing the king and his patriarchy. Isn't independence and self-sufficiency enough? Or is liberation a disguise for your hatred of men for centuries of domination? It is not healthy for you, as a woman, to be liberated from man. God made us as male and female so that, while different, we fit together beautifully. Find him and come home to him. We love you.

However, if after reading this you still think that liberation is the end point of the evolution of the female species, so be it. Please avoid bringing your male "friends" down with you into your separation. Please don't emasculate your male "friends" and their birthright to lead the dance. You have made your bed with ruffles and lace, and you get to sleep in it—alone. If that is the best that you can do, God bless you. Perhaps you will have an opportunity to get the lesson again in your next life.

Character traits are person specific. I trust that you do not nag, maintain senseless rules, exercise mindless changes, or practice deception and coquetry in your relationships with men. If you do, you may wish to reflect on the destructiveness of these practices.

My sincere and deepest hope is that you will use the magic of your femininity and the strength of your self-sufficiency to move beyond liberation to something better. As my friend Mary put it, "Money and power can come and go, but nice (as in a nice guy) is a permanent condition." I trust that you will find him and join with him. It's the elevation of two people to a higher place by virtue of their being together. There is joy and sharing and richness and knowledge in life that can only be achieved with a mate.

Good luck.

"It gives me a headache to think about that boy/girl stuff. I'm just a kid. I don't need that kind of trouble."

—*Boy, 7*

Bibliography

Abell, Richard G., M.D., *Own Your Own Life*, Bantum Books, 1976
Allen, James, *As a Man Thinketh*, Collins, 1974
Bach, Richard, *Jonathan Livingston Seagull*, Avon Books, 1970
Berne, Eric, *Games People Play*, Ballantine Books, 1973
Thy, Robert, *Iron John*, Addison-Wesley Publishing Company, 1990
Bolles, Richard Nelson, *What Color is Your Parachute?*, Ten Speed Press, 1972
Bolman, Lee G. and Terrence E. Deal, *Leading With Soul*, Jossey-Bass Publishers, 1995
Bums, James MacGregor, *Leadership*, Harper Colophon Books, 1979
Buscaglia, Leo, *Love*, Fawcet Crest, 1972
Campbell, Joseph, *Myths To Live By*, Viking Penguin, 1972
Carnegie, Dale, *How To Win Friends and Influence People*, Simon and Schuster, 1936
Chopra, Deepak, *Ageless Body, Timeless Mind*, Harmony Books, 1993
Clark Glenn, *The Man Who Tapped the Secrets of the Universe*, Macalester Park, 1946
Clason, George S., *The Richest Man in Babylon*, Hawthorne Books, 1955
Cornell, Joseph, *Listening To Nature*, Dawn Publications, 1987
Dodson, Fitzhugh, *How To Father*, Nash Publishing Corp., 1974
Dunn, David, *Try Giving Yourself Away*, Prentice-Hall, 1947
Engstrom, Ted W., *The Pursuit of Excellence*, Zondervan Publishing House, 1982
Farrell, Warren, *The Myth of Male Power*, Simon & Schuster, 1993
Fromm, Erich, *The Art of Loving*, Harper & Row, 1956
Gaarder, Jostein, *Sophie's World*, Farrar, Straus and Giroux, 1995
Gardner, John W., *Self-Renewal*, Harper & Row, 1965
Gawain, Shakti, *Creative Visualization*, Bantam Books, 1982
Getty, J. Paul, *How To Be Rich*, Playboy Press, 1965
Goldberg, Herb, *The Hazards of Being Male*, Signet, May, 1977
Gray, John, *Men Are From Mars, Women Are From Venus*, Harper Collins, 1992
Hanh, Thich Nhat, *Peace is Every Step*, Bantam Books, 1991
Hawking, Stephen, *A Brief History of Time*, Bantam Books, 1988
Hardisty, Margaret, *Forever My Love*, Harvest House, 1975
Hartman, Taylor, *The Color Code,* Scribner, 1998
Hill, Napoleon, *Think and Grow Rich*, Fawcett Crest, 1960
Hill, Napoleon, *Success Through a Positive Mental Attitude*, Pocket Books, 1977
Holmes, Ernest, *The Basic Ideas of Science of Mind*, DeVorss Publications, 1990
Jampolsky, Gerald G., *Teach Only Love*, Bantam Books, 1983
Johnson, Tom, *You Are Always Your Own Experience!*, Pathway, 1977
Jones, Robert Llewellyn, *I Love Her, But . . .*, Workman Publishing, 1996
Keen, Sam, *Fire In The Belly*, Bantam Books, 1991
Kopp, Sheldon B., *If You Meet The Buddha On The Road, Kill Him*, Science and Behavior Books, 1972
Krishnamurti, J., *Meditations*, Shambhala, 1991
Lawson, David, *So You Want To Be A Shaman*, Godsfield Press, 1996
LeShan, Lawrence, *How To Meditate*, Little, Brown, 1974
M, *The Sensuous Man*, Dell, 1992
Masterton, Graham, *How To Make Love Six Nights a Week*, Signet, 1991
McWilliams, Peter, *Love 101*, Prelude Press, 1995
Milt John Stuart, *On Liberty*, Appleton-Century-Crofts, 1947
Moore, Thomas, *Care of the Soul*, Harper Perennial, 1994
Melby, Lynn L., *Dead is a Four Letter Word*, Daboey Publishing, 1975

Millman, Dan, *Way of the Peaceful Warrior*, H. J. Kramer, 1980
Newman, Mildred and Bernard Berkowitz, *How To Be Your Own Best Friend*, Ballantine, 1974
Peale, Norman Vincent, *The Power of Positive Thinking*, Prentice-Hall, 1952
Peck, M. Scott, *The Road Less Traveled*, Simon & Schuster, 1978
Penn, Nate and Lawrence LaRose, *The Code*, Simon & Schuster, 1996
Powell, John, *Unconditional Love*, Argus Communications, 1978
Rand, Ayn, *The Virtue of Selfishness*, Signet, 1961
Redfield, James and Carol Adrienne, *The Celestine Prophecy, An Experiential Guide*, Time Warner, 1995
Rifenbark Richard K., *How To Beat the Salary Trap*, Avon, 1979
Robin, Vicki, and Joe Dominguez, *Your Money or Your Life*, Viking Penguin, 1992
Russel, Bertrand, *Marriage and Morals*, Liveright Publishing Corp., 1929
Salk, Jonas and Jonathan Salk, *World Population and Human Values*, Harper and Row, 1981
Schlessinger, Laura, *Ten Stupid Things Women Do To Mess Up Their Lives*, Villard Books, 1994
Sheen, Fulton J., *Way To Happiness*, Doubleday & Company, 1954
Shedd, Charles W., *Letters To Philip*, Jove, January, 1978
Shore, Lee Ward, *Meditations For Men Who Do Next To Nothing*, Warner Books, 1994
Walsch, Neale Donald, *Conversations With God*, G. P. Putnam's Sons, 1996
Weil, Andrew, *Spontaneous Healing*, Fawcett Columbine, 1996
Whiston, Lionel, *Are You Fun To Live With?*, Word Books, 1968
Wignore, Ann, *The Healing Power Within*, Avery Publishing Group, 1983
Zukav, Gary, *The Seat of the Soul*, Simon & Schuster, 1990

About the Author

Randy Smith lives in a resort community in Orange County, California. The author has graduate and bachelor degrees in business administration from the the University of Southern California. He served in the United States Army as an infantry platoon sergeant in Vietnam and was decorated with Bronze Stars for valor and service. He has been president of for-profit and non-profit corporations. He has been active in various community organizations, including leadership roles with an international student business organization, the local country club, symphony, and Toastmasters club.

The author has been divorced twice and has two children, Amanda and Matthew.

Randy says, "I am just a guy, trying to be a man." He can be reached by e-mail at rtsmith@home.com.